Mark Scott spent four decades in the health and fitness industry, with competitive sporting disciplines including junior bodybuilding from the age of 16, over 40 physique competition, extensive charitable fundraising running various marathons including New York and London.

Boxing being his number one sporting passion competitive and as a fan, attending many major world title fights over the past 30 years.

Today his interests are in antiques and the vintage.

Spending time with his family that includes his beloved Boston Terrier dogs is when time is treasured the most.

Dedicated to the memory of my mum, dad, brother David and our Boston Angels.

And also to my wife Tracy, children Liam and Danielle for their astonishing love and continuing care and guidance during the pitch black blindness of my darkest days, a torch that was also carried by our little Boston Terrier's past and present.

My two younger brothers Andrew and James who stood strong and proud in a relentless period of grief for our family.

Mark Scott

POST TRAUMATIC
STRESS AND DISORDERLY

AUSTIN MACAULEY PUBLISHERS™

LONDON • CAMBRIDGE • NEW YORK • SHARJAH

A CIP catalogue record for this title is available from the British Library.

ISBN 9781398453814 (Paperback)
ISBN 9781398453821 (ePub e-book)

www.austinmacauley.com

First Published 2022
Austin Macauley Publishers Ltd®
1 Canada Square
Canary Wharf
London
E14 5AA

My family's encouragement and reassurance that the telling of my story could help others. To Alan Bleasdale for the little gems of advice, I am truly grateful and honoured. David Beckler for his time, help and interest showed in my quest to become an author.

Introduction

In this seemingly ever-increasingly troubled and volatile world, the likelihood of an individual being the victim of a horrific act of mindless brutality, terrorism or violent crime is unfortunately becoming more and more common.

Witnessing the nonsensical taking of a human life, or any form of a life for that matter, can have catastrophic consequences, not just for the primary target or victims but the innocent bystander.

To be a victimised casualty of brutality to the mind, wounds hidden from the outsider looking in, to the sufferer's open wounds that still bleed, that are invisible to everyone except the inflicted, who feel the pain of these weeping injuries, some constantly, some not so relentlessly.

P.T.S.D. POST-TRAUMATIC STRESS DISORDER. This illness was first brought to my attention by an unknowing source, in a song by the music producer Paul Hardcastle, called *19*, released in the mid-eighties. The stuttering chorus line detailed the average age of the combat soldier fighting under the star-spangled banner in South East Asia.

The song described the ongoing struggles US Army Vietnam veterans went through on returning home from duty when the war ended.

Hardcastle brought to the consciousness of the popular music audience, awareness and I think in some people, a diagnosis of the illness P.T.S.D.

Its poignant lyrics resonated with myself, highlighting that I was showing symptoms of this mental tormentor as early as my mid teenage years of the eighties.

Alienation, rage, guilt and suicidal thoughts were all strong emotions used in the narration in the piece of music, excellently accompanied by the music video's pictorial representation. The lyrics themselves depicted the findings by a Veterans Administration Study, after studying veterans' disturbing behaviour patterns.

"Almost eight to ten years after coming home, most veterans were still fighting the Vietnam War."

That was one of the lines in the hit billboard song. The fact of the matter is that most of them were fighting a different war now – a war with themselves.

For most, just like the Vietnam War they returned home from, it was not winnable, the thoughts mirroring the Viet Cong surprise attacks, the ambushing tactics from underground tunnels used by Charlie Victor to ambush off-guard battalions, was much likened to the surprise attack of engulfing, consuming horrors etched into the memory bank of a P.T.S.D victim of the war.

The harrowing images of the war engulfing their thoughts, needing no prompting to resurface for some, like a deadly bullet in the form of a solidified memory, too much for the heavily mentally scarred frontline soldier, the fatal last blow of conflict, would be from themselves, to end up in a body bag, back on home soil, thousands of miles away from the conflict, casualties of the war to suicide, a result of having been left to cope with their horrendous mental tortures when discharged from the forces on their own.

Shell shock was the term given to this condition in previous conflicts, especially in the Second World War. The condition was highlighted when the famous US Army General, George Patton, when visiting an army field hospital for battle-fatigued soldiers in Italy, infamously slapped the face of a soldier who was suffering from the once-called shell shock condition.

In a repeated occurrence some days later, the General did the same to another soldier, who too was exhibiting the same traits of a mentally fatigued soldier of war. His open-handed chastising was witnessed by disbelieving medics attending the stricken patient, which in turn helped expose the high commander's dastardly attitude, bringing with it huge condemnation upon the General. With the fallout from his self-imposed reprimand face slaps, he himself was reprimanded, thus losing his command, and was sent back to a US base in England.

Being part of or witnessing an event that the human brain cannot process, or should I say process so accurately that it's stored in the bottom draw of its physic, repeated in detail, played by the VCR of our brain when encouraged to do so by a trigger associated with the trauma, it renders you in a time warp – a flashback is now the evolved medical term used for this experience.

People experiencing traumas are an everyday occurrence. The development of the mental health illness P.T.S.D is different in many ways, how it affects each individual and how they deal with it. Some are more resilient than others; the immune system to deal with disturbing visions or experiences if you like, are a lot more rigid and don't weigh down on the consciousness like that of the less inferior mentally bolstered individual.

Most people could tell a story about adversity; for some, it's so tragic, it is hard to comprehend how a human being could recover from losses or events that have been bestowed on them.

The witnessing or being part of a horrendous life-changing situation, such situations that spring to my mind, that I'm sure you would call traumatising if subjected to or witnessed first-hand, are:

- A young child witnessing the collision between a helicopter into overhead telephone wires;
- Bullied and stalked as a teenager, by a person with obsessive tendencies;
- Seeing friends' lives taken away in gangland executions, shot, murdered in cold blood;
- Fatal stabbings;
- Cars used as missiles, modified to explode with the intention to kill and destroy;
- The premature death of a best friend;
- Stabbed in the neck, millimetres away from a main artery, beaten, robbed, picked up and thrown unconscious towards the waters of a harbour.

The list could go on and on of people's stories, but the scenarios listed above are not what someone might encounter with some bad luck once in their lifetime, they are a list of some of my own traumatic experiences.

From an early age to the present, my life has been littered with bumps in the road that my mind has had to adjust to.

It is a variety of scarring to my mind, that I open up the partially stitched-up wounds again to tell how I dealt with these life-changing happenings.

I am not going to be documenting the best ways to live a more fruitful life, or how to overcome mental illness and to live happily ever after with no more relapses or set-backs.

It is more about the rollercoaster ride of mental illness, the ups and downs, its strain on the human psyche for the inflicted and the people close to them, and in some cases, others caught up from the inflicted person's actions.

I tell of how and when I should have been sitting down, holding onto the safety rail of this rollercoaster; instead, I was standing up, hands free on its loop.

There is only one outcome on the rollercoaster of mental instability: you fall off if the right precautions are not in place. Illness of your thinking is a white-knuckle ride without the thrills and a seat belt; your reliance is on a vice-like grip making sure at any tipping point you're not unseated.

I liken my mental frailty to a boxer's defence, drop your guard and you're more likely to be caught by a mental punch of intent, like a pugilistic barrage of upper cuts and hooks. Each affecting mental crisis can vary, but you need to know how to block, parry and absorb the concussive derogative mental punches being thrown at you. For most people with mental flaws, some a lot more serious than others, this is not over after 12 rounds, this fight is for life.

The chronicles that follow, depict the effects of the different types of situations I was confronted with, had on my mental state.

The mental torture of being stalked and bullied relentlessly at a young age, to the post reality of being a witness, a bystander in traumatic events I was unfortunate to become part of unintentionally.

The ripple effects of such awful times, that can ignite your mind into conjuring up coping strategies to quell the flood of the recorded horrific memories in the hard drive of your brain.

The desire, the wish to think normally, rationally and joyfully, to find a timeout, to seek out that uplifting pot of gold in your head – euphoria! The easy shortcut is through the treacherous unforgiving mountains of alcohol and drugs, with the very real risk of becoming a slave to these cheating catalysts of joy.

Choices I made, to help cope with what I understand now is an illness, to plaster cast, to bandage the mental breaks and cuts, some right, some badly wrong, if it is possible, to make the reader more aware of how in today's society somebody close could be suffering with some sort of mental illness, hiding it, or not even realising their suffering with a faltering, broken way of thinking.

Accidentally, with years suffering myself, I can now, after unfortunately not reacting to a friend in despair, see the signs of a mental health sufferers quite readily by them exhibiting the traits I once did, and still do, on occasions.

With the likes of social media playing a big part in everybody's life nowadays, the chance that a user could be unwittingly exposing themselves to the germs, in a manner of speaking, that could start mental break down are very real.

Illness of the mind can be subtle in its onset, just like a common cold that could manifest into a life-threatening bout of pneumonia. Symptoms of deteriorating mental health are usually ignored or generally not recognised; that's through my own personal experiences.

Recognising the signs for yourself that somebody is struggling with mental health issues… I myself, a sufferer with problematic mental health, is guilty of not helping friends around me who were suffering, until it was too late, when their cries for help went ignored by me, which resulted in them taking their own life.

It's a burden that I will carry for the rest of my days, and unfortunately it became a trigger for negative emotions to start running riot in my mind; at least I know now it is a trigger and can stop the momentum of irrational thoughts snow-balling.

I now know the triggers or the infectious leaks of thought – well, a lot of them anyway – but some still sneak in and catch me off guard, and the chain reaction begins. The spiral down is quick and fast, and to be honest, like fighting insurgents in a long dugout war, I fight a daily battle with them, and realise I probably always will.

The ripple effect on how a sufferer's illness can affect the lives of other people, ranging just from your mood to your actions, a greater understanding of the different types of illness of the mind, and there are many, to the stabilisation and treatment of the varied conditions, all these avenues need to be explored further and recognised by the general population.

These memoirs of mine are fact not fiction, they are not jazzed up, sensationalised, or distorted to sell a book; in fact, situations told I have actually toned them down and omitted others because I am still not ready to venture into the jungle where they reside.

It is about me, Mark Scott. The first decade of my life which began in a small maternity hospital situated on Trinity Road in Bootle, Merseyside, a small journey away from Liverpool city centre, on the 17th June 1969, and what I would say was a very fortunate start to life.

But from a really young age onwards, situations started to prevail and unfold that made the journey through my life a little bit more trying, should I say.

Every individual deals with certain scenarios in their own way; this is my story of how I dealt with the highlighted situations I write about.

This book chronicles the years of a young teenager being stalked by a predator obsessed with young boy's fledgling muscles.

Witnessing the murders of three human beings, two of whom were close friends, in a gangland execution.

A car bomb attack on my family-run business that engulfed it in flames, destroying it, only for a freak intervention from an iron strut; if not, the whole part of the street would've been destroyed, killing many.

When my demons finally caught up with me, I was being placed on remand in HMP Liverpool for the protection of the public, and me from myself.

The remedies to keep myself from pressing the self-destruct button by raising thousands of pounds for a variety of charities close to me.

Getting attacked on a family holiday, robbed, beaten and stabbed in the neck, missing a main artery by millimetres, waking up in intensive care as the surgeons, with no anaesthetic, sewed up my wounds, but still seven weeks later was able to compete in one of the biggest sporting expos in Europe.

The power of the mind can be awe-inspiring; the flaws of the mind can be catastrophic.

The onset of POST-TRAUMATIC STRESS DISORDER being misdiagnosed by medical professionals, resorting to self-help remedies that I convinced myself were helping me, but over time became more and more disastrous.

My own self-help prescriptions were cocaine and alcohol.

Mental illness is such a taboo subject to talk to someone about, especially decades ago, and even worse if you were male, even to the people closest around you.

The fear of them saying to you, "Oh, what's up with you?" in a negative tone of voice… Or, "What have you got to be depressed about?" were the most common comebacks after my subtle cries for help.

The mountaineering strategy with mental illness, substance and alcohol abuse is a slow climb to recovery, or just stability even, and you do slip and fall, some only little trips, others are major plummets down the gorges and caverns of despair.

I look at myself in the mirror and I know and accept I am a lifer with these conditions. Like a volcano, the larva of my demonic thoughts are thankfully dormant when I am on the right ascent up the mountain, but can so easily become a supernova situation for myself if I become derailed, which I am so well aware of, could be my last.

If this read can be of some help to anyone, even if it's just to prove that other people are suffering in the same way with the same troubling thoughts due to mental ill health, then it was worth the countless amount of hours it has took to the detailing of them.

Please give it a chance. Believe me, I have led quite an unconventional lifestyle, with more ups than downs, which I realise now that I have documented them, unfortunately you're not aware of the positives or the things you should be grateful for when you suffer with the disease of your mentality.

There are many hilarious situations that I hope will give you a smile; I hope so because a smile can go a long way to someone in need of cheering up, as we all know.

I don't mind telling of my stupidity and being the butt of the joke, a chuckle and a smile could be the start of something much bigger, better mental well-being, it certainly did make me smile when I relived them to put to print. I hope you understand and enjoy my time travel through *POST TRAUMATIC STRESS AND DISORDERLY*.

Thank you.

Chapter One
Jaws and the Magic Sponge

The suburban lifestyle and somewhat more rural part of Merseyside was my father's preferred settlement to raise his children. That compared to the inner city flower streets of Kirkdale, his being the cobbled Daisy Street on the fringes of Liverpool city centre, was where he grew up as a child and into a young adult.

Born in 1941, he was introduced to the world by the sound of air raid sirens, as Liverpool was under siege by the blitz of Hitler's aerial bombardment.

With the threat of war looming, my grandparents on my mother's side decided to relocate to the Welsh hills where my grandmother was native. The warehouses around the Dock Road where they lived were just too dangerous to occupy. My grandparents' judgement was completely justified as that area was flattened by the bombers flying in from Germany.

Fifteen days after the Nazi invasion of Poland, my mother was born in the safety of Northern Wales's valleys.

After the war ended, in search for work, my granddad and his family relocated back to Liverpool, Toxteth in fact, until a housing project in the somewhat more leafy, well at least more green, as it overlooked the bunkers and fairways of Bootle Golf Course in the suburb of Netherton, became available, and that is where my older brother and myself would call our first home.

Tragedy would strike though well before my mum and dad would meet. At only 15 years of age, my mum with her two sibling sisters, would lose their father, my grandmother would lose her devoted husband, to bank robbers in a hit and run, who after a heist they had just undertaken, on their getaway route, knocked over and killed my granddad.

I never had the chance to meet both of my grandfathers. My father's dad passed away also before I was born, with cancer, but the way my parents spoke about them, both were great men.

My dad's family's employment, like so many from around the area, was on the docks. My granddad, with my dad's two elder brothers, were dockers, but with the decaying industry in turmoil, people were forced into trying anything they could to make ends meet.

That was the way of life to survive in the city. That was once the pride and the epicentre of commerce for the country because of the bustling docklands, the gateway towards the Americas that welcomed migrants and sailors from all over the world, who were now settled and called it home. The now-swelling population of Liverpool was now struggling to provide employment for its masses.

Being street wise to earn an honest buck, or a dishonest one, was now the primary objective for those who found themselves on the bread line and no longer needed as stevedores, on which generations had depended on.

It was in one of the Merseyside boroughs, Sefton, where my mum and dad decided to settle and bring up their young family, just outside the boundary of Crosby, called Thornton to be precise. That's where we would call home.

The hot summers, the cold winters of the seventies, especially from 1975 to around 1979, were what I can remember being the carefree wonder years growing up.

Fond sporting moments: the European Cup triumphs of Liverpool Football Club in '77 and '78, Emlyn Hughes, captain from the first European Cup triumph in Rome, lofting up the Dumbo-eared trophy, myself replicating the joyous overhead shaking of the once elusive trophy with one of my mother's psychedelic 1970s vases in front of the television.

Purchasing a pack of Panini football stickers, the joy of peeling them apart, the smell of the adhesive-joined paper, carefully placing them in their rightful squared boundary, concentrating intently as not to permanently hang them lopsided for the purpose to fill the glossy album with my football idols of the era donned in the red strip of Liverpool.

The likes of Heighway, Toshack and Keegan, only too willing to do swaps with mates who were Everton supporters when you found that the investment of all your pocket money had bought a Latchford, King or Pedjic in your purchase.

Watching Red Rum on TV win the Grand National in 1977. Aintree Racecourse was only a gallop down the road from where we lived.

I vividly remember running into the garden slapping my backside with my hand, jumping over the flower beds reliving the moment just after Rummy crossed the finishing line.

With the jubilation of being the family member to win our household's annual bet, which my dad would place on our chosen nag every year, a tradition that was honoured amongst our family for years later, at a great price of 7-1. I can recall my winnings being a handful of copper, not quite the return I expected but it was probably my dad's way of steering me away from betting on the gee-gees after the rare win.

Years later I had the opportunity to stroke the legendary horse when he came to my high school in his A-listed decked-out horse box, a guest of honour at our school fete.

Being in the presence of such an icon was truly inspiring. Rummy's demeanour oozed greatness as I gently patted his nose and stroked his neck. I knew I was in the company of something truly special.

The aura that the legend steeplechaser gave off was something that I have only experienced on a very few occasions in my life.

The other moments were when I was in the presence of Mike Tyson as he walked rolling his neck past me, as he made his way to the ring before the only fight he had in England. Believe me, I didn't give Mr Tyson's nose a pat and a stroke of his tree trunk sized neck.

The other was Arnold Schwarzenegger, when after I had competed in his annual European Arnold Classic Fitness Expo in Madrid.

I found myself next to the Pumping Iron revolutionary as he quite strangely undertook the conducting of an orchestra playing the theme tune to his hit movie *The Terminator*. These moments in the presence some of the 20th century's biggest icons I will never forget.

The only worry, of what was my seemingly carefree single-digit years, was that on a Sunday bath night, I would submerse myself into the shark-infested waters of the ceramic tub in our bathroom, where I had convinced myself Peter Benchley's monstrous great white shark was lurking.

Having seen the blockbuster movie in the summer of '76 at the iconic local Crosby Classic Cinema, running out of the showing scared witless after the severed head of the unfortunate fisherman made an appearance in the hole of the hull of his semi-sunken boat, it instantly put paid to my happy, playful splashing around in any type of open water ever again.

My carefree Sunday soak before the schooling week began, was tarnished now with the thought that the terror from the deep was somehow lurking beneath the soapy suds created by the compulsorily additive to any kid's bath time from the period, the deep blue water colouring of Matey Bubble Bath.

My hell time being cleansed was complete with the pungent-smelling, insufferable eye-stinging green shampoo Vosene, which would totally obscure my vision of the harrowing dorsal fin of *Jaws* that I would think was going to break the surface of the foamed blue dyed water of my bath.

The next obstacle to endure was the freezing cold sprint down to the living room fire, the only source of heating in our house at the time, where me and my older brother would jostle for the prime position in front of the warming flames.

Our incentive to face these torments was the Sunday night screening of either *The Muppet Show* or *Black Beauty*, a Tupperware bowl in which I also remember my mum hosting parties for the fashionable, colourful plastic tableware, which would be full of Bird's trifle or tinned fruit cocktail, swimming in the dense sugary syrup coupled with a swirl of evaporated milk.

Our homestead was roughly about 12 miles away from the seaside resort of Southport. There my mum would take us for days out in the summers of the seventies, to the fair ground, the open-air paddling pool and swimming baths.

Going on holiday was very rare, three times in fact, when we were fortunate enough to inhabit a multi-berth caravan due to my dad's commitment to his newly-formed decorating business. Going abroad would not happen till I would turn 21, but these excursions and the rare caravan holidays to North Wales are priceless memories of this truly wonderful period in my life growing up.

My dad's efforts with the decorating business, in which he worked long and hard at, started paying dividends, with a workforce now of around 30 personnel, a new marquee car, shopping sprees to the new trade-only warehouses, where especially at Christmas time my dad would produce rolls of money at the checkout earned through his exploits with his brushes, rollers and ladders.

Surplus funds would enable him to buy his young children high-tech toys of the time, such as Blip, an innovative handheld electronic tennis game. On "Toy Day" at the end of term in my junior school, friends would clamber for a turn on the day's much-favoured centrepiece toy. Children nowadays would give the same device the attention span to last no longer than it would take to switch on an Xbox, or their compulsory smartphone.

At the end of the seventies, storm clouds were gathering in my city and surrounding boroughs – 1979, with the infamous Winter of Discontent; it brought the voters' favourite Margaret Thatcher and the Conservatives into power.

Strikes, walk-outs, outspoken shop stewards and rebellious trade unions, Liverpool was becoming a troublesome hot spot for the Tory government, having in your wallet was now not any surplus money but the card that signified you were unemployed: the UB40.

My dad's business also became a casualty of the economic downturn. A screenplay aired on BBC 2, on one of the only three channels available to select to watch on television at the time, called *Boys from the Blackstuff*, was a portrayal of life in Liverpool so accurate in the way to exist in Liverpool in a Conservative-ran government, hell-bent on keeping the voices of them rebellious trade unions quiet.

But Liverpool was about to get hit again, this time not with the unsavoury policies from the Tory politicians sat in Central London down south, but from the east, the global east, in the form of heroin.

Its evil tentacles started to take hold on the disillusioned youth of the city. This would somewhat silent the people in authority as they tried to cope with the epidemic that was spreading across the city like wild fire.

With a name lost in translation, why such a drug should be given such a glorious title, considering the misery it brought to the unfortunate user; its name and where it originated from was made aware to me by a member of the Merseyside Police Drug Squad.

In a briefing the DS gave to all employees of a new nightspot before opening in Liverpool's docklands, myself being one of them, at a time when ecstasy was establishing itself as a compulsory companion in the nightclub scene, the informative officer's warning of the use of illicit drugs described how heroin in the brutal and savage Boar War, this crude form of opium, was given to injured and severely maimed soldiers on the frontline.

Once under the dragon's wing, all feelings of pain, mental and physical, evaporated. The once unbearable hurt disappeared from the stump of the lost limb, the hurt from the memory of the last battle replaced with visions of waterfalls and rainbows. They then quite willingly returned to face the enemy, and to their certain demise.

Thus each brave soldier was labelled heroic for their super-human efforts returning to the savagery of battle by their superior officers, no doubt sitting safely away in a tent far away from the carnage of war.

The German company who first commercialised the opioid painkiller, Bayer, apparently capitalising on its powerful descriptive words and super-human effects, branded the new wonder drug heroin. According to the superior officers of the Liverpool Drug Squad, that was how its branded name came about. How accurate the story is, I don't know, but coming from a senior police official as I sat listening to him on the top deck of the converted ferry that barmy summer evening in the early nineties, I trusted it to be correct.

With the flood of the drugs, young entrepreneurs from the riot-torn fringes of the city centre found ways to harness their raw skills of business, not encouraged by the schooling they had received to direct it in a more legal manner. Like any commodity in demand, there needed to be importers, suppliers and end-of-the-chain dealers.

These skills of business would put an inner city scally onto the Sunday Times rich list as one of the richest people in the country after becoming the country's kingpin drug dealer, cleverly laundering his proceeds into legitimate businesses.

A community centre situated about half a mile from my home, and in the heart of a council estate, whose occupants comprised of a lot of one-parent families. There is absolutely nothing wrong with the parenting skills from a single mum or dad, but with this three-storied maisonette community, parents who needed to work had to leave their young adolescent kids home alone to look after themselves.

The community centre offered a refuge for them, with activities like boxing, Morris dancing and football, but it also gave the opportunity to discuss tips on joy riding in stolen cars, shop lifting and drug dealing, and any other crime worthy of talking and to get involved in.

The late seventies presented myself with my first non-football sporting arena; it was to put on a pair of boxing gloves for the aforementioned community centre, called the Crane.

The bout was an open-air contest at the local Catholic primary school's summer fete. The makeshift ring was four crow bars, tow rope to make the square ring and the hard patchy grassed school field as the canvas.

My opponent for this three-round fisticuffs was none other than my older brother David. The match makers who were the trainers at the centre, were totally unaware of the sibling connection, as it was only an exhibition bout; coupled with being only 9 years old, underage for a school boy bout, they were a bit lax on the rules of the Amateur Boxing Association.

My brother being 15 months my senior, and with a whole host of his friends watching him, tore towards me in my corner as if he was Marvellous Marvin Hagler fighting for the world title in the open-air car park arena of Caesars Palace, not a Catholic primary school's playing field. His reward for the barrage of punches, was the dislodging of a milk tooth and bloodying my nose.

As the barely padded, cracked leather boxing gloves which had probably been manufactured in the Randolph Turpin era, with my older brother's knuckles lined up inside them, took their toll, my skills of blocking them with my face didn't quite abide with the principles of boxing to hit and not get hit back. A change of tactics was required.

With this I decided to use my extra arm reach, not out of pugilistic know-how, but just out of my survival instincts to try and weather the onslaught till the bell at the end of the round, the bell being literally the school's borrowed fire bell – that operation required the ringer to wind a handle fixed to the big round red alarm.

The biggest, most devastating blows came in between rounds, from my own corner. The added insult to an ever-increasing injury list, was the dousing down I received with the magic sponge, a name given to the big freezing cold soggy sponge used by corner men and football coaches in days gone by to magically revitalise their crocked or dazed fighter or team member.

Nestled in an old tin window cleaner's bucket, the contents included a concoction of water, saliva, mucus and blood from the previous nine bouts. I gazed helplessly up, slumped on my stool, the sponge was submerged into the swamp of bodily fluids and then squeezed on top of my head, this was to somehow rejuvenate me in between rounds.

In round two, my corner man was very impressed with my eagerness to resume battle, but unknown to him, the eager rising from my stool before the bell for the next round was simply to avoid the cascade of extremities being squeezed on the top of my head.

The lasting memories of that summer day was getting led into the first aid tent by nuns, who dealt with my sporting injuries and lectured on how barbaric boxing was; through a quivering bottom lip and saturated face of tears and dried blood, I agreed.

All was worth it shortly afterwards, the bout now a distant memory, as my luck had turned for the better, my natural gift of throwing a ping pong ball were now very much more evident than my jab, bob and weave pugilism skills.

Three flawless throws of the little plastic balls into the target of empty jam jars on a stall in the summer fete, resulted in myself receiving a gold medal, not of a rare metal but one with fins and scales, a goldfish.

My prize was paraded home in a transparent plastic bag, far better than any sporting accolade at that moment in time.

Conversation had now changed thankfully from my ring debut, to the name to be given to my gold medal prize of the fishy kind. Its baptism was easy – Jaws.

Back again too around the same timeline of the late seventies, on a blue sky, sun-drenched summer's day, while pursuing the adventure of capturing caterpillars in my keep-safe jam jar, the whirling rotor blades of a helicopter broke the calm silence in the area of my hunt.

After only just recovering from a previous obligatory rash that went hand in hand with such fieldwork research on these crawly hedge dwellers, my attention diverted to the work of the chopper, whose job that particular day was spraying the nearby crops with pesticides, no doubt to rid the lettuce leaves of my own sought-after prized catch, the caterpillar.

As I watched excitedly the pilot swoop over his desired aim of coverage, he failed to take in account the overhead telephone wires supplying the immediate local residents with conversation, thus creating an inevitable collision on his chosen flight path.

In the developing melee, the helicopter managed to conduct a precarious emergency landing, the lobsided attempt at grounding equated to the extra attachment of sprayers hitting the ground first, flipping it over with somewhat of a bump.

Luckily, it never ignited into flames. I remember looking on in horror as the rescue services managed to retrieve the pilot out of the grounded helicopter, with what I remember from newspaper reports being a broken back.

I suppose the pilot had a very lucky escape considering, probably after a lot of surgery and rehabilitation, he was able to walk in a straight line again compared to victims with mental traumas and a broken mind; they need help just to think straight again, the rehab for that can take a lot longer.

A weight set not of cast iron, but plastic filled with cement, was bought for me by my dad, a purchase made with the thought to help me, as he realised that his son was not of the academic type, who was struggling at school, in an attempt to encourage myself to pursue more of a sporting angle of self-education with the subjects I most liked, in which the better grades from school reports were evident in Physical Education.

With the gifted purchase of the self-assembly dumbbell and barbell set from my dad, it steered me onto a self-teaching quest on the anatomy of the human body and its muscular composition, with the added interest in nutrition. It became a catalyst without me knowing it at the time, that would help forge a future career that would eventually be my mainstay to make a living.

To my own admission, I struggled with my academic schooling as early as my infant years, which carried on all through my classroom endeavours, being placed in the special needs class of my junior school in 1977. A very well pinpointed year you might well be thinking; the timeline stands out due to the delightful memories of street parties to celebrate the Queen's silver jubilee and the corresponding naming of a baby elephant, Jubilee, as our summer school trip to Chester Zoo provided us with a glimpse of their ground-breaking new arrival.

The days spent in the makeshift remedial classroom, a cornered-off part of the assembly hall, generally consisted of watching educational programmes, the likes of *Words and Pictures* or *You and Me*, which used cartoons and puppets to encourage the young watchers to stretch their attention span that little bit further than what the conventional textbook failed to do.

The screening of such programmes would be on a television set that was at least four feet in depth, transported from classroom to classroom on a four-wheeled, high-raised trolley plinth.

The formidable-sized TV that sat precariously on its mantle, if ever it had toppled over, I am sure it would have had the capacity to wipe out half of the class of the educationally challenged children in the blink of an eye that were sat crossed-legged in front of it, probably to the delight of the harassed educator in charge.

I do believe children who found school challenging in the '70s, were very easily overlooked, that was my experience any way. The temporary classroom put together at the start of the day was testimony to the lack of conviction shown towards the academically challenged pupil by the education authorities at the time; proof of such flimsy teaching skills was documented in an end-of-term report of mine:

"Mark quietly wastes his time at the back of the classroom."

I now clearly remember reading this comment, and the effects of it shattering my confidence, to what was already a very quiet and shy disposition. To make such an observant comment just goes to show the lack of teaching qualities this teacher had for her not to act to rectify my weaknesses and to try and help her student under her guidance.

Ours was a bedroom with two bunk beds, for me and my three brothers; yes, you could say space was an issue, but I still managed to use a plot of spare carpet as my own makeshift gym.

The instruction manual that came with the weight set became my daily study book. Now in the early eighties, my prised pamphlet had not been updated to the modern era, as it contained pictorials of bodybuilders from the fifties that resembled the cartoon character Johnny Bravo, but the principles the thin booklet preached about barbell and dumbbell training, had never changed, even to this present day.

As I replicated the movements portrayed in my new schooling textbook, the inspiring physiques of the day, Mr T from *The A-Team*, Lou Ferrigno from *The Hulk*, the relentless pursuit of doing endless barbell curls to sculpture my biceps to mimic the ones Hooper donned as the helicopter pilot in the television series *Magnum P.I.*

My school summer holidays were mainly spent on my own, due to the evacuation of school friends on their summer holidays elsewhere in the country. With a family of four young boys, holidaying away from home was just too much for my parents – keeping a roof over our heads was priority.

My barbell and dumbbell set, with now the addition of a punch bag hung from the large sycamore tree at the bottom of the garden, became my daily companions, where on summer days, workouts in the open air of our back garden were the norm.

This pursuit of physical prowess soon was showing its rewards after six weeks of summer holiday training, on returning to school, my fellow students started to notice a change in my appearance physically and a more confident peer started to emerge from his cocooned shyness.

The strength progression also was noticed by the teachers of the P.E department, thus propelling me into the school's athletic team, competing in the shot put and discus disciplines, representing my school in one of the Liverpool boroughs athletic championships, Sefton, being held at Kirby Stadium, gaining top three finishes in both, a second and third respectively.

The emergence of a young boxer started to grab my attention now as well, whose early career fights were being screened live on a Tuesday night every six weeks or so, on the programme *Sports Night*.

His physique for a boxer, especially for a heavyweight, was more like a bodybuilder. With the host and commentator for his fights, Harry Carpenter, they soon became somewhat of a double act. Frank Bruno was fast becoming a hot prospect in the world rankings and was also moving up my ranks of becoming my number one idol and inspiration.

I would end up following Frank around the country, watching his exploits in the ring. His attempt to dethrone Lennox Lewis at the old Cardiff Arms Park, until finally at a packed old Wembley Stadium, I would proudly, emotionally witness him win the World Title. Sadly, Frank's next biggest fights were going to be with his own mental health, as it started to fail him as he tried to adjust to life without boxing.

Chapter Two
Crosby Health and Leisure

An invitation from a friend whose family had become members of a plush new health club in an area called Waterloo, L22, about six miles outside Liverpool city centre, would be my transition from the weight set in my bedroom to a fully functional gym.

The health club's name was Crosby Health and Leisure. It actually resided in Waterloo, whose borders crossed with the namesake of the gym. Crosby was known across Liverpool as more an affluent suburb of the city; this was quite suiting to the finely furbished establishment.

Still being only 13 years of age in 1983, my membership was given the all clear by the owners, due to the fact that my friend's family had a large membership interest, which I am sure bore some weight on the green light to my consent of enrolment.

The new gleaming plate-loaded machines, which I had never encountered before, the sparkling chrome dumbbells ranging from two-and-a-half kilos all the way up to a weighty thirty-five kilos, were a welcome change to the time-consuming changing of my cement-filled plastic discs I was accustomed to in my bedroom gym.

The rich thick red carpet, the newly varnished pine sauna, wall-to-wall mirrors, where flexing patrons checked out the blood rush into their pumped-up muscle group. Women donned the classic vivid eighties gym attire with compulsory head sweat band, coupled with the iconic leg warmers of the era.

With the head start I gave myself with my self-taught days of pumping plastic plates and reading my instruction manual, fitting into the environment of the self-proclaimed health and leisure club was easy, in which I soon progressed through the ranks of training partners. With my noticeable dedication, I was keeping up and impressing some of the older bodybuilders who took me under their wing.

I was now in my penultimate year of secondary school education, but my real schooling was taking place at the gym. That was my classroom. Work experience for most of my friends in this year would be in a garage, a plumber's or electrician's mate; most of them only learned to refine their tea-making skills for their temporary bosses, rather than how to unblock a sink or wire a plug.

Mine was in the surroundings of this upmarket health club, but to be fair. I had an understanding with the owner of the establishment that my work experience would only consist of myself using the gym to workout.

On the odd occasion I would be asked to stand behind the reception area while she popped out to the shops or went to pick her children up from school, of which I was then shown her gratitude with a box of very crude tasting protein powders or desiccated liver tablets the size of a whole almond, which I somehow trained myself to swallow whole after learning to control my gag reflex, but the gestures were very much appreciated.

By the summer of 1984, my extra-curriculum activity was going to the gym straight after school, as well as spending time in the gym when I should have been in school. With every spare minute, I dedicated myself to pumping iron.

A pastime that most school children did not undertake – to be more accurate, most people never undertook. Not like today, where going to the gym is the norm for most people. These were the days well before the big chain gyms opened up.

My closest school friends had also found their own out-of-school activities to pursue, in the form of experimenting with drugs and other substances – L.S.D, cannabis smoking, glue and gas sniffing, and even some of my very best friends turned to heroin. Even at the ages of 13 and 14, they became victims of this unforgiving epidemic engulfing every walk of life in the city.

I started to be excluded from the times my mates would meet up together because they knew the health freak would not join in on their elicit activities. They knew my stance was firm, I did not do drugs, that was fine with me getting no invitation, as I realised I now had nothing in common with my immediate peers.

In that same summer of '84, my obsession with weight training and bodybuilding attracted the attention of a person whose nickname and reputation would send shivers down the spine of young gym-goers throughout the whole North West of England and beyond.

I can recall vividly that summers night in '84. While sat watching television in the front room of our house, there was a knock on the front door. My mother was in the kitchen. Being engrossed in the TV programme I was watching, I left it to my mum to answer to whoever was on our front doorstep.

The muffled words of a brief conversation between my mum and the visitor I couldn't interpret due to the living room door being closed. It gave me no indication that the visitor was wanting an audience with me.

My mum then entered the front room with what was quite a bewildered tone to her voice, "Mark, your friend's at the door, he wants to speak to you."

Straight away by my mum's demeanour by not saying which one of my friends was calling, raised a curious suspicion within me.

Prizing myself away reluctantly from watching the TV, I stood up to greet my proclaimed friend at the door.

My first reaction was one of surprise, because the person who was stood outside our front door was a complete stranger to me, a lot older and a hell of a lot bigger.

It turned out that a chance meeting with a friend of mine at the top of my road, had sent the stranger to my door step.

The stranger's line of enquiry to my friend was did he know of anyone selling any weight sets around the area.

Being the only weightlifter my friend knew, he told him about me. My friend went on to inform him that I went to a gym, and didn't think I was selling any weights.

After some persuasion from the stranger, he gave the gentleman my name and address.

This innocent assistance from a friend to the weight-set-seeking bodybuilding enthusiast would change my carefree teenage years for good.

The person now stood in front of me was the infamous Akinwale Arobieke, the Liverpool Bogeyman.

Chapter Three
The Liverpool Bogeyman

To the reader unaware of the person standing in front of me, also known by everyone by his nickname Purple Aki, let me put you in the picture.

Standing in the range of six feet six inches tall, with a body weight at around 20 stone plus, his intimidating figure consumed my entire vision, obscuring anything beyond him from my doorway vantage point.

Like most nicknames given out, generally at childhood by your friends and peers for example – a very pale-faced blonde boy from my area was given the title Ghostie – Arobieke was no different. His extremely dark skin tone apparently rendered him a shade of purple, thus Purple became the first part of his nickname; Aki was the shortened version of his given name of Nigerian heritage, his given rightful name being Akinwale Arobieke.

At this time, being the summer of 1984, the reputation of Arobieke had not become one of local and certainly not of regional knowledge yet. A reputation that to date, spans over 35 years. His reign of terror for young teenagers with an interest in weightlifting was only in its infancy on my first acquaintance.

With outstretched arm, he offered his hand for me to shake. I took up the offer, as his formidable sized hand engulfed mine.

Pleasant formalities followed, with the explanation of why he had said to my mother he was my friend, stating people were intimidated by him and it would have been reassuring for my mum to think of him as my mate.

Arobieke's tactic, to ask if anyone was selling any weights, was his subtle way of encroaching his singled-out victim, which was one he would use on a regular basis.

His line of conversation focused on my physical stature, of which he heaped praise upon, then a brief enquiry of my weight training routine quickly turned to would I mind if he felt my biceps.

I considered my biceps to be my best displaying, flexing muscle and didn't need asking twice to show them off. Rolling my t-shirt up, I lifted my right bicep in the usual expected bent arm contracting, tensing manner. The once blank canvas now displayed the evidence of the hours of work I had put in going to the gym to sculpt the now emerging tennis ball looking muscle.

Arobieke then began to squeeze and prod the arm muscle that was now shaking profusely due to the effort of my tensing it for so long, then came the adulation from Arobieke, claiming how big my bicep was considering my young age.

The suggestion was then, did I know what my chest measurement was, and that he could probably tell if he felt my pectorals.

With this unusual touching measuring system, I could feel myself trying to puff my chest out to its biggest capacity, to record the best possible reading my measurer could give me.

Now standing behind me, he cupped my pectoral muscles with both hands and proceeded to squeeze me from behind. The closeness of his odd measuring system was what I would liken to that of a hyperthermia victim: the close bodily contact of another who was trying to raise the body's core temperature of the inflicted shivering individual.

With no exact measurement on release, again he would complement me on my muscular development. His attention shifted now to my leg strength, with it, the description of how he would like to test my muscle groups of the lower body.

As he gave his instructions, my mum protectively popped her head out from behind our front door. "Is everything ok, Mark?"

To which I replied, "Yes, Mum, everything is fine."

Which it was, why wouldn't it be? A friendly fellow bodybuilding enthusiast who was heaping praise on me, recognising my hard-earned gains from the hours toiling away in the gym.

His proposal for the test was for me to bend over while he climbed on top off me as I looked down to the floor. He was face down on my back, with his legs over the top of my head; he then asked me if I could squat his body weight, as he wrapped his arms around my torso with a vice-like grip.

I did what he said a couple of times, bending my knees up and down. He then paused for about 20 seconds as the tightness of his wrapped around arms hold got tighter around me. He then disembarked.

My other fledgling muscle groups – deltoids, triceps and lats – all got the once-over from the sensory touching examiner.

The praising of my strength in his human entangling squat, coupled with the size and firmness testing, seemed to have impressed his judgemental type of scrutiny. With this, he smilingly, pleasantly shook my hand, promising he would call around again to check up on my progress in my bodybuilding quest in the near future.

That was it, my introduction to the one and only Akinwale Arobieke.

That was over 38 years ago, and it certainly was not to be my only encounter with the person labelled by a BBC 3 programme "The Liverpool Bogeyman". That would be screened over thirty years later from my first introductory meeting with him.

Six weeks or so passed, and the long summer days were drawing to a close. A knock again on our front door, but this time I was in the vicinity best to answer the calling. On opening the door, there stood Arobieke, restricting the fading light of the day coming into my home with his immense size.

A friendly greeting ensued, and with it, the enquiry of how my bodybuilding journey was coming along. After delivering his cloak of pleasantries to mask his real motives of intrusive behaviour, he suggested some strength testing, but in a more secluded spot; this was the first real time I felt uneasy in Arobieke's company.

His suggested examination area was in fact the car park at the back of the public house. The pub was at the top of my road. The car park itself was a perfect, obscured, unlit vantage point away from any prying eyes, notably away from my parents' protective gaze, the interruption from my mother on his first visit still obviously in the forefront of his conniving thoughts.

This time the muscle squeezing of both of my biceps was more prolonged. Like last time, his focus then switched to my chest muscles. With that, it was the cupping hugging from behind of my pectorals, adjusting his hand position several times in between each shuffle of his mammoth sized hands a firm grope. My attitude of trying to gain top marks like I had in the previous inspection was dwindling away fast.

Arobieke's thoughts now turned to my thighs, asking if I would tense them for him. His hand then manoeuvred into position clamping around my quadricep, giving it a firm handling, which followed the questioning of was there any improved strength to the area.

The infamous Arobieke squat was the next discipline to come under his scrutiny. Again the duration of the test was longer than what took place on my front door step the first time of asking.

An eerie silence hung in the air, as Arobieke hung precariously on top of me. With the dismount, there was none of the past praise heaped upon me, what replaced the praise was more of a demeanour of his own self-satisfaction; what he had set out to do, he had accomplished.

The feeling that I then got with the hurrying body language he was now exhibiting, was for him to get hastily away from my company, but with a last notification, he gave an approximate timeline of when he would again put scrutiny to my latest efforts to gain elusive muscle tissue.

Picking up his white plastic carrier bag, which I noticed he had on his person the last time, he bid me farewell and disappeared.

The darker winter nights were now just around the corner. An autumn visit came around from Arobieke, his point of contact with me this time though was at the other end of my road. A lone garage situated down a high-fenced driveway, detached away from the house it belonged to. That was where the next examination would be conducted, selected again by Arobieke for its secluded qualities.

Again the wandering hand, squeezing and prodding ritual got underway, but this time I had conditions of my own. There would be no Arobieke squat test, and the time duration would be determined by myself. Suspicions now for Arobieke's real motives for his interest in me were beginning to surface.

But his cunning persistence somehow convinced me to let him to again climb on to my back, to make me undertake his signature Twister game type strength test, the Arobieke squat.

My stipulated conditions were just brushed aside, as his now recognised routine of my muscle geography squeezing from north to south, literally took hold, and with it the usual time duration, if anything exceeding the usual time span.

After this meeting, friends who I had told about of my fellow bodybuilding enthusiast, started to filter worrying information to me. The so-called self-proclaimed bodybuilder was not building his muscles, but building up a formidable reputation as the man who travelled around the Liverpool boroughs feeling and squeezing young boy's muscles for his own fetish purposes.

With the examinations that I had experienced first-hand, the tight pressing of his body he exhibited in the bear hug from behind, the Arobieke squat and the squeezing of my muscles all over my torso, led me to one conclusion: it had to be for a very strange perversion.

Mid November of '84 came around and with it a mid-evening knock at my front door. In a somewhat expected attitude, I answered; my hunch was correct, there he stood with his signature white plastic carrier bag in hand yet again.

My welcome was less inviting, as I tried not to engage in any type of conversation. My strategy was to dismiss any invitation from Arobieke to encroach himself onto me, to politely turn him away; my plan worked perfectly.

As I closed the front door behind myself, a sigh of relief expelled itself from my diaphragm, coupled with a sense of accomplishment that that would be the end of my interaction with this, my own now-growing hindrance; I was to be wrong with that assumption on so many levels.

Disembarking from the bus that took me home from the gym, the stop literally being about 10 yards away before I turned the corner into my road, my mind distracted by the thoughts of my workout that I had just undertaken. The mid November night brought with it the cold and the drizzle of rain expected at that time of the year, when the large looming figure of Arobieke stepped out of the same driveway where he performed his last rendition of scrutiny upon me.

Blocking any more advances towards my home, with a prevailing aggressive nature, he started questioning me on why I had turned him away from my front door days before.

Startled with his obstruction and his demeanour, I explained that my friends had heard whispers, rumours about his real motive behind his infiltration of young weightlifting enthusiasts was more of a sinister one.

With my explanation, Arobieke asked for the names and addresses of the people making the claims about him. He then accused me and my friends of being racists, this claim being totally absurd, which I put to him straight instantly, pointing out that some of my friends had West Indian heritage, others of mixed race. Ironically, it was these same friends who had warned me about his alternative motives of accosting young boys, I told him. That somewhat thwarted Arobieke's accusation of racism.

I doused down the topic of the claims made by my friends by saying it must have just been idle gossip and I apologised for turning him away a few days earlier.

After the reprimand, the focus again switched to my muscular development. Fight or flight hormones were now making the muscles I was flexing for Arobieke's pleasure tremble. My mouth dry, there was no interaction vocally, I just obeyed his commands and hoped the release from his clutches was swift.

As his examination came to a conclusion, the conditions of my release were plain, I should never ignore him or turn him away, tell him of anyone who talked about him in any distaste and then the threat, that if I ever told my parents or others of our impromptu meetings, harm would come to my family.

With the aforementioned list of to do and not to do, brought now a new level of my acquaintance with Arobieke, a level that would change the rest of my teenage years for the worse.

After being instructed I could now leave his presence, the 100-yard walk to my home felt like a 100 miles. Too afraid to look behind me, I finally reached the safety of my home. My life outside the safety of my homestead would now be completely different; it would be one of hyper vigilance, anxiety and fear.

Gone were my carefree journeys to school, when most children worried about if they had packed the correct textbooks needed for the day's lessons, my thoughts were dominated if there was going to be an encounter with Arobieke.

Every time I left the sanctuary of my home, school or the gym, I took up the behaviour of a wildebeest nervously drinking from a water hole, desperately trying to scan the water's surface for any sign of a crocodile targeting it for its next feeding.

Like the wildebeest, I was being stalked by a formidable predator in Arobieke. His threat of violence against myself and my family was a heavy weight to carry on such young shoulders.

I tried my very best not to venture out alone; if this was not possible, I would stay home, isolating myself away, as not to provoke a chance meeting with my nemesis.

Keeping my secret away from my mum and dad was hard. They started wondering why I was reluctant to use public transport now and why asking for lifts to the gym had suddenly become more frequent.

Arobieke over the next 12 months or so was turning up even more frequently, in the morning going to school he would appear, but with the heavy traffic of people around at that time, he preferred his appearances to be in the evening, even better in the darker nights of autumn and winter.

This torment and anguish with the thought of an appearance from Arobieke at any time forged and manifested a new enemy for me to deal with; this enemy would linger around a lot longer though – depression.

On waking up in the morning to going to bed, my mind was consumed with worry and on how I would navigate the day avoiding the company of Arobieke.

With this, thoughts of packing in going to the gym, the only activity, and to a greater extent an education, I really enjoyed, but what would I do or become without my life dedicated to the gym. My future was bleak in my eyes if I was to give it all up, but was it worth continuing, considering the percussion I was under: down to Arobieke? There was also no saying he would not pursue his interest in me if I stopped training with weights.

Dark clouds of the mind started to form in my thoughts. The onset of a bout of depression to myself was like a creeping effect consuming me not just mentally but physically. The muscles of my face would start to sag, a decrease in energy because my brain activity was only producing thoughts of negativity. A huge pressure, an invisible force above you that pushes you down. Communicating becomes ever so hard and speech becomes slurred.

The only way to shelter myself against this dark cloudy weather system was to sleep and hope that upon on waking, the sun had come out. Unfortunately, this storm sometimes reaches inside the shelter and into your dreams – there was no escape.

Good days would come and go, but then I noticed a pattern forming. The days I never went the gym, generally because I couldn't face the torment of the journey, I would be a lot worse, so to combat this, I never missed a workout. Braving the Arobieke mind field, I started training as often as possible, at least six days a week was the norm, with now an added session of boxing on a Sunday morning with a friend who boxed as an amateur locally; unfortunately, in the next few years, he would become a user of the drug sweeping across Liverpool, heroin, which abruptly ended his pugilism days.

The Arobieke reputation and somewhat of a folk law was also sweeping across Liverpool, not just amongst his preferred intended targets of young gym goers, older people had now started hearing about him. A genuine fear was building up, and this was with people who had never even encountered Arobieke or had laid eyes on him, but for me, I was at the top of his hit list.

Being a victim of the muscle squeezing giant filtered through to children going to my school. They would then tell their friends in other schools. Within no time at all, I had become known as the bodybuilder who knows the muscle-squeezing Bogey-man personally – a victim would be more precise.

On meeting new people, conversation would quickly turn to my relationship with Arobieke, somewhat ashamed due to the fact his reputation was based on him feeling and touching young boys. With the threat of harm to my family still at the forefront of my thoughts, deflecting the intended route of discussion would always be my objective in these situations.

Older children, the kids with reputations of being tough and with some school yard fighting backgrounds, started to talk and befriend me, with it offers of confronting him. With a self-preservation attitude now adopted by myself, I surrounded myself whenever I could with this human shield.

Even with this self-imposed peer protection, somehow he was always be able to ambush me when I was alone, catching me at my most vulnerable.

Arobieke would continue to perform his touchy feely routines. My attitude, still with a scared disposition, was changing into a reluctant one as well. I got a feeling that he knew my patience was wearing scantily thin.

A few days later after an encounter with Arobieke, barking from our faithful family dog Max alerted me to look out the front window of our house. Being dark, I couldn't see anything at that moment in time to concern me, but Max never barked for no reason, our Kerry Blue Terrier – legend has it that the breed originating from the county of Kerry had kissed the Blarney Stone over on the Emerald Isle; Max, however, would've rather sank his canine teeth into anyone or anything that threatened his family human pack.

As my dad went to his van the next morning, someone had stabbed all four of his tyres with a knife. Bemused with this attack on his van, he could not think why someone would target him or vandalise his property, my father had no enemies. But I did: the bully, the tormentor, and with this act now, the coward Arobieke.

Still with no idea about my now hostile relationship with Arobieke, I never suggested who I thought the perpetrator could be, with no one who had a bad relationship with anyone and the only person who had threatened violence against me and my family, the number one suspect had to be Arobieke.

In my eyes, this brought my threat of a more likely attack to me personally to a new level. If it was Arobieke who had vandalised my dad's van, I knew now he carried a knife.

This cowardly and mindless act of property damage somewhat started to change my totally petrified way of thinking towards Arobieke, to one of hatred and anger. When the opportunity presented itself, I would seize it with both hands to stop the torment once and for all. I was at my wit's end – enough was enough.

This opportunity to face my enemy on a more even playing field would be in fact just around the corner. A chance gathering of the older children that formed part of my human shield presented itself one evening; the position for a skirmish would be perfect as well, at the top of my road. I couldn't let this chance of defiance pass me by.

Arobieke's intentions were clear as to what he was in the area for, as a lone associate of our group came breathlessly running towards us. In an attempt to get his words out, a mixture of nerves and gasps of air, he relayed his message:

"Aki wants a word with Scottie."

To my delight, I was not alone for the first time in a confrontation with Arobieke. With this, I gave the rallying call to the troops around me who had previously offered their services.

All of them gave me the green light with their assistants to gain some retribution. A show of force hopefully would bring an end to this awful period of bullying, worry and uncertainty.

The only chink in my cunning plan was that the posse gathered, my knights in shining armour, apart from myself and the messenger had never clasped eyes on Arobieke before.

The illuminating glow of a street lamp gave my boy gang of vigilantes their virgin glance of the silhouetted figure of Arobieke as his emergence into view slowly presented itself.

My eyes now fixed onto the shadow of our intentions. Pace gathered from a slow walk to a calculated trot of engagement.

"This is it, lads, let's do it," was my war cry to my makeshift battalion of young enthusiastic warriors.

The silhouetted figure that was creeping into view began to reveal its solid form. Our vision was locked onto the full enormity of our foe. There was no going back now; my time of destiny with Arobieke was here.

As I gave the final ushering call to my assembled unit of overthrowers, I looked over my shoulder to wave on the decisive charge.

My arm flopped down from its once rigid state, like a flag that had lost the power of the wind to keep it fluttering. I was greeted with the fading sight of the soles of the training shoes, of my now retreating army, running away in the other direction.

The deceleration of bravery was rapid. The realisation engulfed me instantly that my monumental effort to dethrone the tyrant that was Arobieke, was going to be futile.

With literally nowhere to run, my solo charge left me in the firing line of the enemy. My energy, like my companions', had also deserted me, like a car that had ran out of gas and with flat tyres, I was rendered motionless on a lonesome highway. In front of me now was an angry Arobieke.

"What is your plan now, Scott?" Arobieke snarled.

My speech was the third absconder that night. With no reply, head bowed, I had already waved the white flag of surrender, without a punch being thrown.

With his expected volatile reaction to my rebellion, my only way to diffuse the precarious situation I found myself in was to let him once again pursue his anatomy squeezing ritual without any resistance.

This time, it would be at the back of a row of shops, in an entry just across from my road, dark, quiet and perfect in every way to conduct his agenda of examination he was formulating in his disturbed mind.

It felt like an eternity before I was released from his clutches, somehow amassing just enough energy to get me home, which was probably not much more than a hundred yards away. I scurried off like a rabbit that had escaped the sharp talons of a preying raptor.

My burrow was the safety of my bottom bunk in my bedroom, where I cried myself silently to sleep.

Chapter Four
Bright Lights and a Dark Night

Leaving school in the spring of 1985 at the age of 15, with the expected dreadful examination results, sixth form or college was out the question; I just didn't make the grade. My own form of higher education was already in full swing: the gym.

Learning and progressing fast, it was suggested by the lady owner of the gym at the time that if I ever had any aspirations of competing as a bodybuilder, I should go to a well-known gym in the Bootle area of Liverpool to seek the advice of a well-known bodybuilding guru.

A date and time was arranged for me to have an audience with this knowledgeable adviser. It was in early January of '86. Snow was falling hard on the evening in question.

I thought of this as a possible safer passage, with less chance of having to endure an Arobieke examination due to the weather conditions disrupting public transport from the south end of the city where Arobieke resided.

My assumption of an Arobieke free journey to the gym in Bootle was correct; the blizzard conditions worked to my advantage. The entrance to this famous weightlifting institute was a steel plated door just visible because of the snow that was drifting either side of it.

Not knowing the etiquette of entrance to the gym, not wanting to enter unannounced either, I gave the sheet metal door a couple of hard knocks.

An obliging gentleman opened the door dressed as what I can only describe an oily lumberjack, complete with woolly hat and garden gloves, being more suitably dressed for logging in Alaska. I asked him in a rather sheepish voice if he could please tell me where I could find the proclaimed muscle flexing master. He pointed over to an elderly bearded gentleman putting one of his patrons through his training regime.

As my eyes wandered around the gym, the dress code seemed to be in line with the person who opened the gym door for me. I now understood the layers of thick clothing, with the hand and head wear, was due to the fact it was colder inside the gym than it was outside in the blizzard conditions.

Handling the cold iron without the protection of a glove could well have fused bare skin to any of the steely plates or gym apparatus seemingly crudely forged to torture the user into submission.

It was a rude awakening to what I was used to in my plush, neatly organised and heated health club. My balancing skills were tested as I tripped and stumbled over discarded dumbbells left by the previous users until I reached the vicinity of the gym proprietor.

Introduction complete, he went onto suggest conducting our discussion on bodybuilding, training and dieting ethics in the warmth of his high-rise apartment building just around the corner from the gym.

After scraping the large amount of snow off his car with a yard brush, the stone's throw journey to his place of residence complete, I was invited into his flat situated near the top level of the building.

With his abundance of knowledge on the subjects of nutrition and anatomy, he gave me a master class in bodybuilding, like music to my ears, absorbing every droplet, I somehow processed the information easily, much easier than my days of schooling in the conventional subjects of arithmetic and English language.

An hour or so passed, learning more in this time span than I would say in the whole of the last year preparing for my CSE exams.

Then came the acid test, a visual one from my examiner, in which he asked me to strip down to my boxer shorts, so he could give me the final yes or no, whether or not I was ready with my muscular development, to deplete my puppy fat on a strict dieting regime, with the notion to exhibit my physique on a competitive platform.

Thoughts of failing this visual examination were just too overbearing, as my nerves took hold. I struggled to untie my tracksuit bottoms and fumbled with my training shoes laces. My unsatisfactory high school grades the previous year flashed through my mind as a reminder of my struggling inability to learn successfully.

His eyes scrolled up and down my presentation of my juvenile muscles, just as if he was overlooking an examination paper from a pupil who had just handed him their final dissertation; my appraisal would come a lot sooner than negotiating a multi-page document.

My nonchalant attitude towards the result of my appraisal did not mirror the joy I felt inside me having passed the scrutiny of a nationally renowned physique judge. With it came the green light to single out a competition of choice so I could prepare diligently on the correct diet and training plan.

The target, now identified, was to be in a British championship qualifier, in the 16 years old or under category, to be held in Middleton, Greater Manchester, in the late February of 1986, which was roughly about seven weeks away.

Implementing a strict dieting and training regime came easy to me; discipline wasn't a problem. My focus was driven to achieve at least a placing in my rookie bodybuilding outing.

With this dedication and determination, the ever-constant thoughts of Arobieke accosting me abated slightly, clearing of the dark storm clouds – a break in the depression.

In its place, was now an excitement that I had not felt in a long time. Every workout gave me a lift in my mood, coupled with the clean diet, spats of euphoria would service as my physical change mirrored my improved mental clarity.

I returned to the gym in Bootle once a week so my adviser could access my progress, educating myself on every visit about the world of bodybuilding and the lengths competitors went to on how to present the best physique possible on the day of competition.

Homework of mastering the art of the compulsory set of poses that I would be asked to undertake on stage by the appointed head judge, having gone through them in my newly acquired posing trunks in the freezing cold conditions of the gym, it was now up to me to perfect them at home in my bedroom.

Dieting jargon of carbohydrate, sodium and potassium loading and depleting, were all on the agenda to learn, so as to implement them in the final days of my preparation.

It was like a fast-track degree in nutrition and bodybuilding science. Every minute detail was important, a personalised posing routine to music.

Removing my manhood down that had took me 16 years to harvest, buttering myself with hair-removing cream, standing in the bath holding a crane karate stance due to the smearing of the pungent smelling cream under my arm pits, with my patience gone, using my dad's razor to banish the remaining bristles of hair down the plug hole.

Then the application of false tanning foam, which the colouring at the time was more consistent with an Oompa-Loompa than of a deep Mediterranean tan the bottle suggested.

The day of the show soon came around. The six or so weeks of strict dieting and training had paid dividends to my physical appearance. I was ready to engage in a bicep battle with teenagers from all over the country.

Still in my thoughts was Arobieke; would he track me down to Middleton to attend as an unwanted spectator?

A plus for me was that my chaperone for the day, a fellow member of my health club and a training partner, just so happened to be a police officer. He also knew about Arobieke through his job with Merseyside Police, as he was now on their radar, presumably because of complaints about his bizarre behaviour.

The venue, Middleton Civic Hall, was now filling up with spectators and fellow competitors, when the call for all the teenagers in my class came over the microphone, to make their way to the changing rooms to prepare to go on stage.

The designated area to get prepared was packed with eager contestants, frantically curling dumbbells in a desperate hope they just might encourage one last growth spurt to each muscle, young teens man-handling bull workers as if their life depended on it, all to achieve the required pump, to inflate each muscle group to the max.

My nostrils were greeted to the quite overwhelming smell of self-tanning cream and Ralgex; with the more-than-generous applications of these products, it had created a mist, stinging my nostrils and eyes combined.

My chaperone helped me to oil up, which meant to coat myself liberally with baby oil, to give my muscles a nice glossy finish. As I went through the process of pumping up, a quick scan of my rivals already stripped and ready, a new wave of confidence oozed through me; in my eyes, I was realising I had a decent shot at winning the title on offer.

Stepping out in front of an audience felt great, better than any of my other previous engagements with a crowd watching me intently.

My other under-the-spotlight appearances included being a shepherd in my junior school rendition of the nativity, where I proceeded to fluff my lines, putting the whole ensemble of young shepherds and angels into total disarray, to the amusement and horror of the parents in attendance.

The local schools swimming gala was another, where I nearly drowned in the wake of my faster rivals, coming in last to a round of applause from spectators in sympathy to my embarrassing attempt at the back stroke.

My erratic spin cycle splashing of non-coordinated strokes would have probably thoroughly cleaned a pile of dirty washing if it would have been thrown on top of me in my dire attempt to perform the desired swimming discipline.

Like my boxing debut previously documented, the above debutant appearances also ended up with family and friends uttering the somewhat now familiar comments, "It's not about the performance or the winning, it's about the taking part."

It was never any consolation hearing them famous last words after every public showing of mine, the shame and embarrassment would always keep me to the side-lines until my bodybuilding debut.

As each contestant in my category was announced by the compare, I proudly stood facing into the blinding stage lights that obscured my vision of the packed auditorium.

My number, name and gym where I trained was relayed to the spectators to a warm round of applause. The hardest pose was trying to smile constantly as I was advised to do, the muscles of my face ached as I awkwardly smiled, resembling more of a grimace than a smile of confidence.

We were then given our instructions by the head judge. The other officials then cast their critical eye over each and every one of us, the dozen or so teenagers flexed and grimaced to the commands relayed to them through the microphone.

Then came the first comparisons that were not in numerical order, that gave an indication of who was in the running for a podium finish. Three numbers were asked to take one step forward from the rest of the line-up, as the surge of adrenaline seeped into my bloodstream on the realisation that my number was amongst the three asked to take that giant step.

I now had an inner confidence never experienced before by myself. Gone was the scared boy afraid to walk down the road. A bright sky above me shone in the form of stage lights that had dispersed the clouds of depression I had been suffering caused by the Harpy-like torment from Arobieke.

After the set rounds of posing and the individual routines were complete, all our efforts, off stage and now on stage, it was now out of our hands and in the hands of the judges assigned to the task of placing us in order of merit.

Every contestant received a medal that was placed over our heads. As I lifted the grey cast medal with red ribbon to inspect it, my breathing was deep due to the intense pose down a few minutes before, twinned with the growing anxiety of my imminent fate.

Doubts now started to filter into my way of thinking; how would I react to a bad showing? Would I just go back to life of hindrance from Arobieke? Had all my hard work and sacrifice been in vain?

I glanced over to the table laden with the trophies to be handed over to the first three in each class. I brushed the doubt and uncertainty aside for once in my young life; I knew one would be mine.

Six competitors were asked to stay on stage, the rest to leave, a thank you for their participation ensued.

I was in the top six; to me, still not good enough. As descending placements started to unfold, my confidence was now at a pinnacle, as the compare reached the top three, again not satisfactory, I desperately wanted to be at the highest height on the podium, I was good enough to grace it was my attitude.

Two competitors left, and I was the other half in the equation. I had done it, convinced I was to be crowned the best teenager bodybuilder on that day.

In second place, the pause seemed as if time had stood still. The now quiet auditorium all waited for the result. The two quivering youngsters were the focus of the whole gathering of bodybuilding enthusiasts' attention, then it came – "From Crosby Health and Leisure, Liverpool, Mark Scott."

The somewhat mix of applause and cheering was solely not for me, as my fellow competitor and his followers realised he was the victor that day. Despondent like an ungrateful child receiving a gift for his birthday he didn't want, I accepted my trophy, with it an invitation to compete in the British finals at the end-of-year Winter Classic. I left the stage like I had just been chastised and sent to bed.

Back in the changing room, already the autopsy of my second place had taken over my thoughts; where did I go wrong? How could I rectify it in the finals? My companion for the day came to congratulate me and to offer his, probably a biased one at that, opinion that I should of won.

With a lump in my throat, trying to hold back tears of disappointment, composure was in order, to reflect on how well I had actually done in my first ever competition, a re-routing of my train of thought, brought now a sense of immense accomplishment, with that, the journey back home to show the hardware off for my endeavours to my mum, dad and brothers. It was a great feeling, as I proudly placed the trophy on top of our television, pride of place so everyone could see.

It would be ten months of hard training to gain more vital muscle tissue before the finals in that December of 1986. A focus, again a distraction from my pursuer in the form of Arobieke, but a head-on confrontation with him in the summer of that year would be to some extent, a life-changing encounter.

A quiet period of non-intrusion from Arobieke was down to my perfected stealth like behaviour going to and from the gym. What did continue was the slashing of my dad's tyres. After such occurrences, I would be told of sightings of Arobieke in the area, the same night as the vandalism, again reminding me the chances of it being this menace were high; more to the point, a knife-wielding menace.

It was now the early June of 1986. The completion of my daily workout complete, I left the gym to walk to the bus stop on the nice sunny summer evening. A lift home on this particular evening was not available, but being so pleasant, it encouraged me to chance the journey home.

As I waited for my red double decker form of transport, a bus on the other side of the road that had just come from the direction of my home, had a friend of mine yelling at me from an opened sliding window on the top deck:

"Mark, Mark, Aki is waiting for you at the top shops by your mum's, he is going to get you."

My blood ran cold; I could not believe it. Out of all the nights I was alone. I picked up my training bag and ran as fast as I could back to the gym to see if there was a willing Good Samaritan able to escort me home.

My predicament explained to a few including the gym personnel on duty at the time, fell on deaf ears. Fortunately, a friend, a couple of years older than myself and an ex-paratrooper in his thirties who was aware of my history with Arobieke, came to my aid, but my heroic army veteran's plan was not just to see me safely home, it was for me to confront my nemesis one to one, with them waiting in the wings, reinforcements if necessary.

I had heard of a similar cunning plan the previous year; this time I was very reluctant to put myself in the firing line. With my experience of reneged battle strategies, to go through with this plan was even more ambitious. For me to go head-to-head with my enemy alone, just the thought of it was absurd.

The battle cruiser, driven by my regiment leader, powered into the coordinates given by my friend that was travelling on the bus less than thirty minutes before. Just as my look-out patrol had reported, there he stood, in the doorway alcove of the butcher's shop, opposite the entrance to my road.

We slipped past undetected and parked up out of sight around the corner. There we made our final battle plan, with plenty of objections from myself regarding the first wave of attack. I was just too scared to face this man monster alone; I was a juvenile at 16 years of age, he was a fully grown adult possibly with at least 8 stone or more weight advantage.

My co-conspirators put belief in me that this was the only form of deterrent against Arobieke. That I alone should confront and stand firm against the bully that for the last two years had made my life a misery, with the reassurance not to worry, they had my back.

Petrified and shaking, my mouth now as dry as the summer's day itself, I set off on my mission, looking back constantly to make sure there was no repeat of my last failed overthrowing, when my troops retreated to leave me stranded alone.

The evidence of Arobieke's presence in the recess of the butcher's, was given away by his immense size as I caught a glimpse of his favoured form of holdall, a white plastic carrier bag draped from his huge hand.

One last glance back at my backup to make sure they had held there position, I moved into the zone where the enemy would detect me, which he did immediately.

With an aggressive and demanding tone of voice, he spoke, "Scott, I want a word with you."

With this, I turned and faced the command. My reply, "Do you?"

As he stepped down off the step of the doorway to grab me, I launched a pre-emptive strike. My right hand clenched at my waist, it now hurtled towards its target: Arobieke's face.

Flush on the cheekbone, it landed; the result, a wound that seeped blood straight away. "Scott, you're dead!" Arobieke raged.

His vocal counter-punch delivered, mine was a double jab, which was far more effective than his threat. My instinct of hands up, work behind your jab and be first, was quickly breaking down the once invincibility I thought Arobieke had over me.

A feeble kick was his form of retaliation, which I easily avoided. Again with my constant offensive tactic, my repeating left jab peppered the target, followed by my right back hand.

This was becoming a lockout on the judge's cards if there had been any, but what there was were two friends, who with the visual encouragement of my progress, joined in the one-sided melee. Coming from behind, they jumped on to Arobieke's back in the process trying to pull him to the floor.

The size and strength of Arobieke rendered this ploy insufficient as he shrugged of my two backups. We now found ourselves in the layby that ran along the row of shops, holding our subject against the side of a skip that was just so positioned there, we pounded away at any vulnerable part of his body.

The now brawl spilled onto the main road. This was happening at peak hour in broad daylight. As the traffic came to a halt, a bus carrying some very observant passengers and acquaintances of mine started shouting, shall I say, encouraging remarks to beat the living daylights out of him.

Adrenaline now fuelling my actions, I was pulled back by my paratrooper friend, "That's enough now, Mark."

It was not nearly enough for me as I yelled at Arobieke, "Come on! Come on!"

With the now abated attack, Arobieke dabbing his bleeding facial wounds with a handkerchief, he issued his chilling warning, "You're dead, you, Scott!"

With pats on my back on our retreat for my valiant effort, I was driven to the safety of my home by the commander of our three-strong posse.

In my adrenalin-fuelled and flustered state, I had to tell my parents what had just unfolded and why. The relief of informing them of my secret that I had kept from them about my situation I had put up with for years, was now in the open.

The threat against me I took seriously, what I was certain of was there was going to be some sort of retribution from Arobieke, more likely sooner than later.

As darkness fell, I prepared for what I thought was going to be some sort of cowardly attack on our home. In my defence, a hammer, which I placed at hand's reach under my bed, as evidence suggested in the vandalism of my dad's van, if Arobieke was the culprit, he was armed.

Going to bed that night, fight or flight hormones were still evident in my bloodstream as my melatonin that regulates our biorhythms struggled to send me into a peaceful slumber.

I opened my eyes from my bottom bunk, trying to quickly separate the noises I so vividly heard from being reality or was I still in a dream state of imagining the alarm sounding bark of Max, our Kerry Blue Terrier.

The three loud bangs coupled with the smashing of glass, the scrambling sound of feet, as my parents jumped out of bed awoken by the disturbance; the anticipated attack was underway.

I reached for my chosen form of protection, the hammer; my older brother dropped out of his top bunk and grabbed his 7-iron golf club. We propelled ourselves downstairs not knowing if the enemy was ready to engage physically in our home.

My dad was already downstairs frantically assessing the damage from the attack, my mum in tears cradling my youngest brother, who was suffering with one of his severe asthma attacks that had previously forced him to spend time in Liverpool's own children's hospital, Alder Hey, with his condition.

This entire event, visual and its audio, is imbedded into my psyche that plays today as clear as it did like on that 1.05am early summer morning in 1986.

The damage and threat assessed quickly, three full set bricks had been propelled through the front windows of our house, damaging furniture on their trajectory before landing in our living room; the four tyres on my dad's van, slashed, rendering the vehicle useless.

With this, the thrusting of a kitchen carving knife into my hand by my dad, only too willing to swap it from the hammer I was already gripping firmly, with it the voice of a family embraced in its self-preservation, my dad issued the battle cry to me, "Finish him, Mark, finish him."

The feelings I felt as the door was opened widely for me, my older brother and Max the dog, I can only describe as what soldiers must've felt in the First World War; I am surmising as they left the safety of their trenches, bayonet in hand, to the cries of charge, as they headed towards the frightening abyss of no man's land towards the enemy, to kill or be killed. A conviction of my intent was solidified in me, to end the life of another human being.

This primitive, barbaric and truly frightening emotion, if I can summarise it like that, is one I never ever wanted to encounter within myself again.

In a calm and calculated instruction to my brother, I told him that I would engage with the enemy first, and not to swing his 7-iron aimlessly, so to avoid him hitting me under friendly fire.

As we looked to the top of the road, we saw the unmistakeable figure of Arobieke turning around the corner, not willing to face us in combat, in a war he instigated two years previously, with a fourteen-year-old boy.

The junction of the road quickly was underneath us, as we caught the sight of the fading tail lights of a car, no doubt inside of the vehicle, the guilty party of the cowardly attack, Arobieke.

My now relaxing muscles and the receding fight or flight hormones of cortisol and adrenalin, that my endocrine system had been secreting, gave my mind time to reflect on the seriousness an encounter with the enemy would have been.

Being at a point where my mind was in a fixed state of evil to end a life, was a one-way decision, not like the crossroads I found myself at the top of the road.

I had been prodded, poked and cruelly teased into a corner; was I to slide down that corner, put my hands over my eyes and curl up into a ball, just to let it continue?

No, I did not, standing up to my bully, like my veteran paratrooper had advised, was now looking back probably the right thing to have done, for my situation any way.

Standing up to your tormentor, bully or someone making your life unbearable does not necessarily mean to physically confront them, share your torment with someone; everyone despises a bully, everyone, period.

Your torment is instantly halved by sharing your misery and your strength is doubled. I cried silent tears for two years, by not telling my parents or anyone else the extent of my loneliness in the world of the intended prey of a predator.

Missing out the carefree teenage years of my childhood, excluding myself away from my peers, locking not just myself away socially but mentally. Silence can be deadly; talk, just speak, and you will be heard.

The scars of this traumatising episode in my life were not visible on my skin, the igniting of my indigenous survival hormones during this event left an invisible stamp on my mind a lot longer than their secreted output.

The mayhem that prevailed that early morning and the evening before, if a positive was to be taken out of it, was I felt somewhat of a transition from boyhood to manhood.

News filtered around the neighbourhood and back to the gym of the whole incident, from the toe-to-toe trading of blows, to the attack on my family home. My two compatriots decided to lie low understandably for a few days; my attitude was different. The fear I once felt for this human being had evaporated and solidified into an overwhelming hatred, that every minute there on, I planned his demise.

A counter attack was now an option I was hell-bent on carrying out. Within days I had located the address of Arobieke; it was in the Southend of the city, Toxteth to be precise. Arobieke, originally from Manchester, not native to Liverpool at all, had based himself on the outskirts of the city centre.

My gallant efforts against Arobieke had not gone unnoticed; I had debunked his myth of the untouchable, tough, man monster that the rumours had of him. Offers of assistants from new recruits in my now war with Arobieke was welcoming, knowing that I was at last not alone in my fight for living a more stable and normal existence.

A friend's car provided the transport for recognisant missions, to find out about the best angle of attack on his place of residence and on him. A time and date for a stake-out to catch him was pencilled in, and then some very disturbing news broke.

On the local radio station, headlines of a young teenage boy being chased onto railway lines in Birkenhead across the River Mersey being electrocuted and killed was their top story running that day. A man had been detained in connection with the incident and subsequently charged with the young man's manslaughter. The young innocent victim was Gary Kelly; the accused was none other than Akinwale Arobieke.

Chapter Five
Bowls of Blood

Arobieke now behind bars, my own incarceration behind the high walls of uncertainty, of intimidation and scaremongering started to crumble. What lingered though were nightmares, visits of Arobieke in my dreams, similar to the cult horror movie of this time period *Nightmare on Elm Street*; my Freddie Kruger was Arobieke.

Even while awake, loud bangs, the breaking of glass, even the barking from my faithful canine companion Max, brought a sudden vision of playback to me of that awful night me and my family had endured.

I now made the most of my newfound freedom, most of it travelling to and from the gym, now not having to rely on lifts and chaperones. My adventuring optimism spread to walking further afield more frequently than before and using public transport. I embraced every free step, roaming without the constant state of hyper vigilance that had been instilled into me due to Arobieke's ever-looming threat.

The health club where I had been a member for the past three years went through a transition period during this time, evolving from a plush members' club containing mainly chrome shiny dumbbells, machines that held only a moderate maximum weight stack and a sauna that some patrons solely came to use, to a gym that could cater for the most avid weightlifting enthusiast, due to the change of ownership in the late summer of '86; a local and nationally successful bodybuilder and his girlfriend at the time became the new proprietors.

With this came the offer of my first permanent job: the resident gym instructor. The knowledge of training and nutrition that I built up over the past few years set me in good stead for my new career. My total devotion to read and listen to anything to do with the subject gained me a plethora of information ahead of others at the same young age.

The collaboration of my new job and training for the finals of the 16-year-old British Bodybuilding Championships worked well. I decided to get some more competitive experience on the advice from my new employers, so mid-way through my preparation for the finals, a friend of mine, Eddie, drove me down to Crewe in Cheshire to compete in an under-21 competition, the South Cheshire Juniors.

I was totally out of my depth in my advised spontaneous choice of competition. The added age difference was a factor, myself being only 17 years of age, but there was something else, something they must be doing that was far more adventitious, something that I didn't know or was not aware of.

Their young physiques were incredible, a lot more muscular and a lot leaner. I was dumbstruck by their appearance and somewhat despondent by the experience; my despondency would become even worse a few weeks later at the finals.

The Winter Classic was what the finals were titled, the same civic hall in Middleton, Manchester the venue. The procedure like before started with the pumping up in the changing rooms and the application of baby oil to give that glimmering sheen under the strong stage lights.

Before I applied my stage sheen, I gazed around the frantic, push-up muscle-tensing opposition to see what I was up against. There I noticed a fellow fanatic from the previous competition. He never placed in the top six that day; to be quite judgmental, I had him holding up the bottom three placing if being truthful. Today was a different story.

The transformation was astounding. I could not believe this was that same person some 10 months previous. He had far surpassed my muscular development. It was not just him, to my dismay, with this accelerated muscle fibre growth spurt, most of the other trailing contenders from the last outing had sprinted past me and left me in their wake of advancement.

The troubling and hot topic of conversation between these mini Mr Universes were what they had used to achieve this metamorphism – anabolic steroids.

At the tender ages of 16, 17, and in some cases even younger, they had resorted to the testosterone mimicking drugs, instead of relying on their own indigenous testosterone naturally getting seeped into their bloodstream at this pinnacle stage of their boy-to-man transformation.

It was a subject I knew nothing about considering my time served in the sport. My naivety, or to be more relevant my innocence and strict policies on any genre of drugs, had cost me a shot at this prized goal of mine.

Keeping my stance on drug use and reputation intact, especially at such a young age, was more than what a plastic trophy was worth to me. It did not feel like it at the time to be honest. Leaving the stage and taking the only thing home was a once brightly coloured pair of posing briefs, now stained with the fake tan and baby oil once covering my deflated muscles, but more to the point, my deflated ambitions in the world of muscle flexing hobbyists.

Deflated yes, but I put on a brave face knowing I could still hold my head up high, in the fact my strict health-conscious reputation was still unblemished.

My 18th birthday came and went. Thoughts of progressing higher in the sport of bodybuilding were still a firm objective of mine, especially now having trained and been around not just some of the best bodybuilders in the country but in the world.

My employer at the time ushered in my services to help him train for a professional contest that was held in New York City every year called the Night of the Champions. A contender for the British Heavyweight Bodybuilding title also asked me to join in his preparation for his stint at the prestigious title.

With world-renowned bodybuilders visiting the gym to train when on tours of the UK, the likes of Lee Haney who held the coveted Mr Olympia title at the time, Tom Platz, renowned for his extreme leg muscularity, Gary Strydom the giant South African, a big threat to Haney's Sandow trophy, and Bev Francis who was the subject of the film *Pumping Iron 2 The Women*.

I listened intently to their training and nutrition philosophies, as they relaxed in our reception stroke refreshment area above the gym.

The other subject I started researching avidly was P.E.Ds – Performance Enhancing Drugs.

This subject now was a must learn, to understand what they were for starters, the different types of P.E.Ds, and there are many. Listening to people I looked up to as mentors gave me valuable and honest advice. I was lucky I had some of the most knowledgeable people in the business to pick their brains, like my employer whose advice was to steer me away from the temptation, the lure of the artificial hormone.

One particular word of wisdom from him, was that bodybuilding success would never come from a pill or injection but from being blessed with the best genetics from your parents and a lot of hard work.

I had the latter but on the genetic side, I was naturally tall and slim, suited maybe to other sports, but this was not just a recreation for me, I now found myself being in a far better frame of mind when I was constantly training and eating clean. It was without really knowing, it was my own form of medication to stop the storm clouds of depression rolling in.

The choice was ultimately mine and mine only, whether I was to follow suit into the not-so-natural progression of using anabolic steroids to further my body building aspirations.

The decision I thought long and hard about, but in the January of 1988, I decided to take that giant step and break my illicit drug virginity.

After making inquiries regarding requiring a legitimate product, I decided after much research and advice to start with the mildest form of anabolic steroid on the market.

With minimal side-effects, safe enough for even a female to use, it had the lowest androgenic properties of any anabolic, meaning it exhibited low testosterone traits such as aggression, oily skin causing acne, hair loss, and would not hinder my own production of indigenous testosterone.

You may well wonder why on earth would I want to take such drugs labelled performing enhancers given the possible side-effects, even in such a low dose. It was because my carefully researched, hand-picked P.E.D delivered good anabolic properties, meaning it helped utilise proteins better, thus repairing the broken down muscle fibres that resulted with weight training.

A pyramid system of taking the tiny white tablets was prescribed for me by a credible adviser on the subject. The frosty January morning of 1988 was my self-administration starter date.

It was a real ground breaker for me. A glass of milk was the aid to help the process along nicely. As I looked down into the palm of my hand, nestled in the middle were the magic beans of muscle construction.

With a three, two, one countdown in my head, I swallowed the pills. Firstly, a sense of immense guilt engulfed me; I could not now retrieve my status as never having taken an illegally governed drug, one that should have a GP's signature giving it the legal go-ahead.

I felt dirty; I felt I had let my parents down with their ideologies on drug taking. Composing myself, I reinforced the reasons on why I had taken this path. These reasonings prompted more positives than negatives, but they still didn't stop the thoughts that my head was going to fall off or some other hideous side-effect related to my consumption of the tiny pills.

The duration of the course on this anabolic steroid was approximately 8 weeks, during which time I did not turn into a raging Mr Angry; my hair did not start receding and falling out, but it also didn't turn me into a teenage Arnold Schwarzenegger, which to be honest, was a disappointment.

I had trained hard, eaten correctly as usual, but nothing happened miraculously, which I could put down and say that it was because I had delved into the world of the P.E.D.

Given it was literally a tickle with the weakest form of anabolic steroid, the curiosity on the subject was still in the forefront of my mind, so more research was undertaken. The only literature available at the time was from medical journals, but that only gave information about usage for the ailments for what they were actually manufactured for.

However, there was a handbook at the time that seemed to be a reference guide for athletes and bodybuilders alike. Finding the up-to-date information on all types of P.E.D available on the black market and how to administer them into their cycle, this book seemed to be the go-to at the time.

The advancement was to combine other steroids – stack them, is the preferred term used. This was the progression I took, again with very minimal doses. The introduction of intra-muscular injections also became part of the cycles.

With time, coupled with a lot of hard work and dedication, changes to my physical appearance started to gain pace.

My bodyweight increased greatly as well as my muscle mass. At now 19 years of age, I was approaching 17 stone plus, sporting nearly 18-inch biceps, but – there was a but, a big but in these size increases: side effects, side effects I was totally unaware of.

At first I thought my low mood was down to my delicate mental state still lingering after the years of torment from Arobieke, but after a noticeable pattern formed, after more in-depth research it was also documented as a side effect, it was quite clear it was down to the use of the artificial testosterone.

Roughly two weeks after the completion of the course, a noticeable drop in my mood would occur, and depression would set in.

The research stated that with the use of non-indigenous, testosterone the body's natural supply of testosterone would diminish, so when finishing the administration of the artificial form of the hormone, the body was at a much more lower level state. In some cases, the testicles' function of production of testosterone had ceased totally; I was aware of this but the resulting depression I wasn't.

It was awful. The depression had my head in a vice-like grip. I would become withdrawn, get very tired quickly and lethargic; all these were so very counter-productive to actually what my ambitions regarding my workout schedule should have been like.

The other troubling side-effect that occurred during the cycle, was – even more serious than the depression in respect to how bad they became – nose bleeds.

My workout journal became the first stained victim of my tap-like bleeding nose. One drip splattered the document detailing my day's gym visit. In seconds the drip became more of a pour from both nostrils, rendering the aforementioned page of my training diary to the bottom of my waste paper bin.

I tilted my head backwards to try and somewhat avoid any more blood coverage over my bedding and bedroom carpet. I quickly started to choke on the amount of blood I was dispensing from my nose, as it was now rerouted to the back of my throat as this became the new channel for the blood to flow freely.

In a bloody balancing act, I headed for the kitchen downstairs to get the washing up bowl so I could gather the gushing blood flow collectively by hanging my head over it.

Now back in my bedroom, the bowl in between my knees, it started to fill up rapidly. This situation was now starting to worry me, as I swirled the bowl around as if I was panning for gold. The dark red blood was now filling up to a quarter of the plastic bowl's available capacity. The pour then slowly subsided to a steady drip and then to a 20 second or so plop into the bowl.

I stealthily crossed the landing to the bathroom, gambling that I would not come across any family member, to pour the contents of the bowl down the sink without having to explain how and why I had enough blood on my person to happily satisfy a vampire's family picnic.

This type of episode would not just happen in the comfort of my bedroom but in the most awkward and embarrassing situations possible – walking down to the shops, on the bus, even serving customers with protein shakes in the gym's refreshment area; I remember trying to stem the flood of blood from entering one customer's post-workout shake but failing miserably, turning his yellow banana shake into looking like a ripe strawberry flavour.

As soon as I felt the warm flow of blood trickle to my mouth, it was a scramble to grab my forever handy pack of tissues, which on some occasions would not be enough and a towel would be the only fitting padding for the job.

Haemorrhaging from the nose I then discovered is a common side-effect with the use of anabolic steroids; severe haemorrhaging had even been reported contributing to fatalities.

I recall reading one such article in a popular bodybuilding magazine called Flex. A teenager of a similar age to mine at the time, suffered such serious haemorrhaging; his body went into shock and he died.

This now was becoming an issue that I had to seek advice about, but going along to my GP was out the question. The reaction of such a health professional would have understandably been to cease such self-administration, then would come the uncomfortable source of questioning of my supply and the legality of me possessing such drugs, that was just too much of a sensitive subject for me to address.

The credible sources of information available to me for advice all pointed towards seriously thinking about my use of continuing on the drugs, but it was a catch-22 situation for me; without them, it was virtually impossible to compete against people using P.E.Ds.

I was now not just putting my health at risk, but possibly my life. The more I educated myself on the use of these drugs, the realisation that there was a smorgasbord of side-effects possible if taken in the wrong way and not for the purpose they were manufactured for.

My overwhelming desire to follow a competitive bodybuilding lifestyle was starting to fade, but I just wanted one last crack at a regional competition, to use P.E.Ds and see if I could stand in a line up and hold my own, knowing I had levelled out the playing field.

I was still classed as a junior under 21 years of age and would be for the next two years. Time was on my side to slowly progress sensibly, not like what I was hearing other bodybuilders were doing by staying on their chosen steroids permanently.

The plan now was to try and train as natural as possible over the next few years, implementing my choices of P.E.D sparingly, twice a year was the mapping of my use, which was very minimal compared to others. Monitoring the bleeds and depression more carefully would be the gauge for overuse, while adopting more preventative strategies to avoid more possible ill effects.

At the age of 20 the noticeable gains in muscle mass due to the use of anabolic steroids also came at a cost physically and mentally

At sixteen years of age weight training and competitive bodybuilding was a huge help to overcome my systematic bouts of depression

Chapter Six
The Return of the Bogeyman

In this period of generally moving on with the other normal things in life – work, relationships, aspirations and goals for the future – my self-experimenting with P.E.Ds and training continued, then came the news of the release back onto the streets of Akinwale Arobieke.

This came as a bitter blow to my now fairly relaxed former anxious hyper vigilant state, the local radio and newspaper were the only sources of information at the time to find out about Arobieke's intended court appearances and release dates due to his appeal against the charges of manslaughter.

Venturing out alone again became a strategic effort of avoidance, but things had moved on within myself, I had grown up fast from that scared school boy of a few years ago, still imbedded in me was the hatred and detest for this person, putting added testosterone to an already raging fire of anger literally put me in a more delicate, explosive frame of mind, which I realised had to be governed rationally.

My feud with Arobieke had now spread to the attention of the local police station, realising this became evident on my two encounters with him shortly after his release; the first incident, the first eye contact with him since the events of '86 was him waiting at a bus stop just out of the immediate area of our toe-to-toe battle. On seeing his presence, it was hard to control my instant reaction of not just to launch in with every bit of harnessed energy of repulsion to satisfy my troubled mental state, with visions of my mum and younger brothers brought to tears still vividly playing in my head because of the actions of this man.

Instead, I quickly ran home to get my older brother to bolster my offensive, with the history suggesting he possibly could be armed with a knife. I put a pen knife in my pocket which in those days was quite normal to have such an implement on your person; I actually bought this particular knife from the toy shelf in the newsagents at the top of my road years before.

As me and my older sibling approached Arobieke from the other side of the road, a police patrol car screeched in between the two parties, the constable getting out from his car to firstly speak to Arobieke. After a short discussion with him, the constable headed towards me and my brother.

His first words startled me a bit. "Hello, Mark, we are just making sure there isn't going to be any public order offences about to happen here."

The constable knew my name. The conversation then turned to an accusation from Arobieke that I was carrying a knife, Luckily enough, on the appearance of the police, I slipped the pen knife into a hedge. The officer relayed the accusation to me but answering it at the same time stating, "You haven't though, have you, Mark?"

With this, he then instructed me to just go home and that he would deal with my sworn enemy.

The second appearance was outside the gym itself, a late afternoon showing coincided with a nearly full gym with friends and members alike, bewildered with Arobieke's bare-faced cheek. I marched to confront him by myself, raging this time. In toe, which I did not know, were half the gym's occupants as well, equipped with a host of iron bars and heavy objects that were destined for Arobieke's attention.

Again, screeching into position, a police patrol car this time with blue lights ablaze, intervened just in time again.

The same knife accusation against me ensued. The two officers again obviously knew about the hostilities between me and Arobieke. Defusing the volatile stand-off was handled well by the police officers, then came the friendly words of advice by the police that it was in my best interest to avoid any altercations with Arobieke. A watchful eye was on his movements and any type of vigilantly type or personal vendettas against Arobieke would be not tolerated.

With the two rapid interventions from the police, it was certainly obvious Arobieke was under the watchful eye of the law, which in some way helped me relax slightly more and in turn helped to abate the sheer infection, the disease of the mind I had to harm a person to a point of committing a crime of unimaginable consequence, by losing my liberties and my life as I knew it.

To have more of a focus at this point of time was pivotal to my own sanity, so I decided to aim to compete in that one last bodybuilding competition. My choice of event was the North West Under-21 regional contest, to be held in the June of 1990.

So at the turn of the new decade, my preparations began. Throwing myself into this totally one-tracked train of thought brought again a somewhat peace to my fragile mind, my vivid recollections, flashbacks of being apprehended by the predator who had been the bane of my life for the past six years, the inability to talk about it, with this blinkered approach hopefully the depression would be less demobilising as well.

The regime of training and dieting intently, being in a place of definite, visually seeing the progress brought happiness to me. I was in touch with all my senses reasonably and not overloaded to a point of anxiousness, paranoia and frightfulness that had plagued me for the best part of my teenage years.

The impromptu nose bleeds continued, but with the strict dieting regime, not overloading on salty foods I think certainly helped. Bleeds were now gated into heavy lifting sessions, predominately leg press, squatting with weights touching the 500lb mark and heavy barbell curls, which was a favourite of mine to perform. The pressure of these heavy effort movements certainly opened up my inbuilt pressure valve in my head to a cascading fountain of blood.

The show date came along quickly. If I was to conclude had the P.E.Ds helped in any way, it was obviously an overwhelming yes.

My body weight on stage was over 15 stone lean, or the term used in the bodybuilding circles, ripped. At 6 feet 1, and at 20 years of age, they were impressive stats, but were the consequences of the risk factors regarding my physical and mental health worth it, was probably an overwhelming no.

On show day itself, a not-so-welcome spectator was present in the foyer as I registered in as a competitor – Arobieke.

My employer at the time and the promoter of the show itself had a friendly word in his ear that I was there to compete, and that any unwanted distractions from the likes of himself, he would be instantly ejected from the building.

I was so focused on the job at hand, his presence held little prominence in my thoughts. I had no intention of him spoiling my day on stage like the way his intrusive bearing had played on me for years.

After all the literal blood, sweat and tears, I was crowned the Junior Under-21 North West Champion 1990 that day. It was a great feeling when my name was announced as the winner but then the realisation, that this was just half the job done. The British Finals were at the end of the year and to be honest my genetics for the sport put me at a disadvantage; the drug use would most certainly have to increase, with that no doubt more unpleasant side-effects.

I had put my whole life on hold for the desire to win a bodybuilding contest, coupled with my restricted teenage years due to Arobieke. Maybe it was time I lived my life and saw the world; I had never been abroad at all at this point. Aspirations of moving to California for a year or so were my ambition. I had already started to buy dollars with any spare money I had.

But my first port of call would be Ibiza; the rave scene over there was just getting started, so me and two mates from the gym had booked a two-week excursion there two weeks after my 21st birthday in the July of 1990.

One of these gym goers, I would forge a great friendship with. Over the next few decades, we would spend a lot of time growing into our adult life together. The young man was roughly the same age as myself, his name: Robin Blundell, aka Bungie.

In the late eighties, I supplemented my gym instructor income with work on a Saturday night, firstly at a night club as a bouncer in Wigan Lancashire. Most of the security personnel travelled from Liverpool to work in this very busy night spot. There I was introduced to a young employee of the club who was from the area, who I started dating.

I would also work on the security of major bodybuilding events around the country, with work opportunities arising to also work on pubs and clubs around Liverpool as well. These placements of work would certainly bring funny, strange, violent and tragic situations to the helm of my work experience undertaking in this genre of employment.

Dating steady now, my girlfriend Tracy became pregnant and gave birth to our son Liam in the November of 1991. Like any new parent, the protective bond you have with your new-born is natural to all human beings.

This protection I seriously had to control when seeing my worst nightmare in front of me when pushing my new-born son in his push chair one Saturday afternoon whilst out shopping.

As me and my partner pushed our new-born son through the shopping arcade, there standing back, just observing the general occupants of the arcade was Arobieke.

A cold, numbing feeling of shock and horror proportions took over that manifested into the same disturbing emotions that I never wanted to feel again since this same person attacked my family home. One single hostile action from this person towards me and my young family, would have no doubt ignited animalistic parental instincts of which the consequences would have been complete eradication of the threat, I am totally convinced of this.

Ushering my partner and our precious baby away in the opposite direction, I turned and noticed Arobieke's attention was directed to some new unbeknown victim, a young boy roughly the same age as I was on my first encounter with him. My heart was beating out of my chest and my stomach was trying to regurgitate its last meal with the nausea feeling I was trying hard not to overwhelm me.

This self-preservation was now just not about me with Arobieke, my new family and their safety was now my utmost concern.

Chapter Seven
Moving Up a Class

Stepping back a few years momentarily, the late eighties brought an introduction to a different type of class for myself. Class A drugs, anabolic steroids classification was C at this time, a new recreational drug was flooding into the big cities of the country, in turn into the clubs and bloodstreams of the club revellers, the revellers would even be re-classed themselves, into ravers, the clubs into raves – ecstasy, or M.D.M.A, had arrived.

Another illicit drug which only wrapped its tentacles around a certain class of person who could afford it, which deemed and contained its use to the champagne Charlie type of club-goer, the celebrity, a politician or a successful sports personnel, was cocaine.

Cocaine had its foot under the table a lot sooner for its more select users than its new same class compatriot ecstasy. My hard stance of using such a class of drug would be dismantled in just one drug-fuelled euphoric night in the early spring of 1989.

My wall of defiance against any type of drug use I would certainly say was weakened by my explorations into the world of anabolic steroids. The softening and subtle subsidence of the aforementioned foundations, made the plunge into this unforgiving territory a lot less questionable and less guilt-ridden.

The night in question was a Thursday evening in the April of '89. A gathering of members and friends of the owners of the gym at a local public house owned by a regular gym-goer, was to be a farewell good luck salute to my employers who were embarking on a new business venture in the Netherlands, thus leaving in charge of the running of the gym in their absence, to the responsibility of myself.

Midway through proceedings, another gym member stroke friend arrived, with it an increase in tempo, laughter and revelling as this person took centre stage. This person's demeanour, personality and his presence in a room was really quite unique; his name was Kevin Maguire.

As the night was coming to a close around 10.30pm, Kevin suggested if I was interested in prolonging the night and heading into Liverpool City Centre with my employer's eldest son. Merriment down to the alcohol consumption, which I never really undertook, only on occasions like the one I was in, persuaded me to go along on this mid-week quest of frolicking.

Kevin the instigator to the extended excursion into the city centre, was an all-round good sportsman, short in the way of height, he excelled in his chosen sport of Judo, competed as a bodybuilder in his youth, participated in other martial arts, was a good long-distance runner, in a later part of his life found a passion for rugby as well. His other attribute was his fearless temperament and when switched on, quite a savage and vicious one.

With these credentials, his notoriety all over Liverpool was well documented, which in the years to come, I would witness first hand.

We sped towards the city centre in Kevin's life-long partner's silver Mini Metro Turbo. The car itself was a wolf in sheep's clothing in its performance as it hurtled through most of the red traffic light signals on route to our first anchor point, The State Nightclub.

With a friendly and mutual respectful greeting from the front-of-house security personnel, his attire all black, with black leather gloves and walking cane, himself a very well-known figure in the Liverpool underworld. We were gently ushered through to the long hallway avoiding the queues, before heading to the big grand doors, the entrance to the once hosting hall for avid ballroom dancers.

As the grand doors parted, I did not realise how well the antique bespoke hinged entrance shielded what was actually happening on the other side, the light now seeping through the ever-widening gap, coupled with the noise bellowing out of the huge sound system. Cascades of multi-coloured lasers and strobes had the occupants of the ballroom in a trance as they vigorously, energetically danced to a more upbeat mixed version of popular billboard tunes of the time.

The highly charged sustained efforts of these clubbers was something I had never experienced before; whistles, glowing sticks, even some patrons donned what I could only describe as nuclear radiation suits.

It certainly seemed if they were powered by such a power station judging by their efforts not just on the dance floor but on the chairs, tables, even the bars had severely passionate deranged disco dancers on it. What was fuelling the over energetic dance moves, I thought to myself, they certainly were not intoxicated with alcohol so what was powering these danceathon revellers. I was soon going to find out.

Feeling quite positively awkward among the sign language of big fish, little fish, cardboard box, squeezing hugs, positive handshakes, all from complete strangers that any long-lost bosomed pal would have found over the top.

My guide for this clubbing experience, Kevin, was quite a celebrity amongst some of the patrons, who, shall I say, were like modern-day versions of Al Capone's entourage of the 1920s. As I was introduced to these acquaintances of his, an exchange took part with one of them, Kevin being on the receiving end of the exchange.

As Kevin's co-conspirator left our company to join the masses of jubilant jiggers, the closing of our trio together in a huddle, to the command of, "Open your hand up," from Kevin.

I opened the palm of my hand, a grey speckled tablet was placed snug in the middle of it, with the further instruction of, "Just swallow it," Kevin instructed.

I did what I was told.

Naively, I never questioned what it was that I had now going down my throat proceeded by a lukewarm glug of beer from the bottle I had been holding for the entire duration of being in the club.

The heat of my hand had made the hob's alcoholic liquid an ambient temperature, that made the process of swallowing more challenging, but not as challenging of that of my peripheral taste buds picking up the pharmaceutical notes of the tablet on its entering journey from mouth to stomach.

After an eye-squeezing swallow, I questioned Kevin what was it I had just ingested, "It was an E, Ecstasy," my educator replied.

My look was an acknowledgement of understanding, but really I was still totally bemused with what I had just participated in. Not really knowing what I was to expect, I waited for the reported effects to take hold.

Updates of our tablet's progress into our bloodstream bounced between the three of us. "Can you feel anything yet?" was battered about more than once between us, until suddenly my chewing gum I had in my mouth disintegrated, evaporated.

My jaw started to literally vibrate. Before long, my teeth were chattering as if I had replaced my own set of nashers with a set of the key-operated wound-up teeth from a joke shop.

With my free hand, I tried to control the embarrassing situation by holding my bottom jaw as I tried to order drinks from the bar, as the giggling barmaid tried to make head and tail out of my requirements from the vibrating speech being admitted from my mouth.

I turned around for some assistants from my company of friends, only to see the pair of them now embraced in a hug and on release made dance moves like a bumble-footed muffin bird. I seriously needed to get back to them because my body had started to gyrate to the rhythm of the night.

I awkwardly walked/danced back to the strictly come two left-foot dancers, emptying my three bottles of alcoholic beverages with a cascading foam of beer in the process erupting over myself and anyone in my path.

The three of us now were being overpowered by clandestine waves of euphoria, prompting adventurous dance moves, that at the time we thought mirrored the choreographed moves of The Jackson Five. A more realistic analysis on witnessing such ambitious dance routines would have been that of The Three Stooges, suffering from seizures due to the intermittent switching on of the strobe lighting.

Also embodied within me was the need to hug or shake a complete stranger by the hand that came into close proximity of me. I realised now what the passionate greetings entering the vicinity was fuelled by.

The time came to pull anchor from this particular venue and head on to another suitable establishment, that with the right type of music we could carry on our first ever raving experience.

The venue pin-pointed to us was a snooker club in the Toxteth part of the city, The Pivey Club. 3am swung around in the blink of an eye, as we arrived outside the snooker venue, a queue already formed around the building which was already full to the brim inside, as we again got ushered straight into the foyer.

My first reaction again was of shock, as the proposed sport which it was dedicated to was not at all in any form being played. Each individual 12-foot snooker table was now just a raised plinth for about half a dozen or so revellers to strut their dance moves on top of.

The hour hand of the clock seemed to speed around like the seconds' hand. 7am was looming, with it the realisation I had to be in work at 1pm, not just with this deadline, the departure of my employees to foreign shores and my responsibilities that came with it.

Slightly flagging now, this didn't go unnoticed by some of the personnel I had been introduced to that evening, of which one suggested to follow him into the office of the snooker club. Inside the room were the expected furnishings of an office of business; the business of this person was quite different though, his was cocaine.

On the desk in front of me, heaped in a pile, a pale yellow lumpy powder, that was positioned in the middle of a mirror, with it a rolled-up twenty pound note and a Stanley knife-blade.

The streetwise looking gentleman who led us into the room leaned over the aforementioned mirror and its occupants and artistically pulled an amount of powder away from the mother pile and began to chop it up with the unhandled blade, separating it into the required number of lines for the room's occupants.

With an outstretched arm, he passed the rolled-up paper currency to me.

"There you go, kid," he said.

"What is it?" I questioned.

After my non-query attitude hours before, I wanted this time to know exactly what was being dangled in front of me.

"Charlie coke," was the reply. "Proper Peruvian flake," he added.

"Not for me, mate, thanks," was now my stance.

Knowing very little about the drug itself on offer except that it was highly illegal and dangerous, I declined the first offer, then came the reassurance of go on it, we'll sort you out for the day.

My guard now severely down because of the other elicit substance in my bloodstream, I reluctantly accepted. A failed attempt to snort the powder up my nostril without closing the other resulted in a tutored demonstration.

My second attempt was successful. Little did I know this would become a pivotal moment in time for myself, that I would repeat continually over the next thirty years.

With the initial diminished tiredness, with a surge of confidence and intent heading into the day ahead, we left the snooker club.

What was all the bad reports and health warnings about with this drug, I thought to myself, I was in fact experiencing only feelings and emotions I had been wishing, craving for, during the past few years of low esteem, shattered confidence and the suffering bouts of depression.

A mask was shrouded of what ultimately would have been a totally exhausted sleep-deprived body and mind, just like the instructions that came on the packet, it had sorted me out.

Then came the crash, hard fast and with a bang. After completing most of the first day of my new responsibilities with ease, the last few hours remaining on the clock, plus with the added duties I had to undertake after my regular hours had finished, the hands of the clock seemed to have ground to a halt, as I constantly clock watched.

A creeping thought started to encroach on my thought pattern, if only I had one more line of the power powder to get me through the last unforgiving hours of sheer exhaustion.

So there it was, in my head, kidding me already that it was something to lean on in my hour of need, either for a fatigued state, a low mood, or a boost of a superlative charged energy enhancer.

With just one tiny line of cocaine some 12 hours previous, it had me virtually under its spell straight away.

Over the years, I have known people to try the modified coca leave, and never found the satanic lure of the South American export appealing, thus never going back to the devil's dandruff again, but for me and my brain chemistry, even with my firm stance on such drugs, it suited me like a tailor-made Savile Row suit.

Due to my vulnerability regarding my mental health, this self-prescription would have a place on any self-diagnosis I found my mind struggling with in the decades to come.

Unfortunately, the desired effect of correction with any of the diagnostic mental states I tried to remedy, would simply worsen over time, even multiply, just like germs on a putrid dish.

Chapter Eight
Jaffa Cake Fights, Heinous Nights

The late eighties/early nineties brought an explosion of recreational drug use amongst every one of my friends and acquaintances. The rave culture had people of all adult ages, from all backgrounds, experimenting with these so-called party drugs.

People who I would have never expected to, including myself, all were dipping their toes and getting caught up in it. Not just at a weekend but every day in the week, there would be a venue exploiting and only too willing to host nights that would encourage drug use in Liverpool City Centre and surrounding areas.

My extra cash generator from the late eighties and into the next decade was working on such venues on the security side at a variety of establishments. Having a young family now to support the cash supplement became a staple part of my income as well as my main source of wages I received from the gym.

The placements of doorman work were at various pubs, clubs, private member establishments, even on a converted ferry named the Manxman that had a permanent mooring in the Waterloo Dock, Liverpool. Its two floors were now splashing out melodies, not splashing through waves on route to the Isle of Man, its original intended course of duty.

A private members' squash club in the quite affluent area of Crosby, also had me on the payroll, where the posh subscribers of the racquet ball club would get drunk and let their hair down after the local pubs in the area had squeezed out every minute of their legal opening hours.

So onward the drinkers went to their reliable squashy sanctuary, where it wasn't a small rubber ball bouncing off the walls, it was themselves due the more often than not a drunken stupor.

These two mentioned establishments had the watchful eye of my introductory chaperone to the rave scene, Kevin, as the deterrent against any unwelcome personnel causing a headache to the management and owners alike.

His reputation itself would usually be enough to ward prospective trouble-makers away. If it didn't, they were then usually tracked down and visited – in one such case a kidnapping charge was brought against Kevin; it ended up with him spending a lengthy custodial sentence for the offence.

All the hours I spent working in these types of venues brought all types of situations to my awareness, some farcically hilarious, some terribly disturbing and some downright heinous.

I could quite easily document the experiences of warring factions of security companies around this time, the battalion of guns and armaments I would witness being held behind the scenes, the confiscated drugs and knifes, the riots of rebellious revellers and religious communities, to the brutal fights where body parts were actually bitten off in such skirmishes, where bottles and knifes would maim and severely scar individuals for life, but so would probably most security personnel or employees of these venues at this time be able to relive such events.

But what I will tell you, is two different extremes of my time working the night shifts on such places, the first in the squash club, private members only establishment, the second a shift on an all-night dance club in the docklands of Liverpool named The Hard Dock.

The latter would disturb my delicate, soft human personality, in turn reignite mental fragility that had somewhat been contained for a short period of time, but let's start at the farcically funny, not the down-right heinous.

An introductory telling of how the running of the hours spent on the front door of The Crosby Squash Club on a Friday and Saturday evening is probably appropriate to express the story adequately.

The Squashy, as it was fondly known around the local vicinity, held an extension to the normal hours of selling alcohol that all the other public houses inside the boundaries of Crosby did not have; this was granted due to the private members licence it held.

These couple of extended hours to buy alcohol made the upstairs of the courted, ball-smashing premises a magnet for late-night drinkers, but and it was a big but, they had to be a member with a valid membership card to gain admission – no card, no entry.

The establishment was also a place of interest to my friend Kevin Maguire, his formidable reputation coupled with his capability of warding off potential trouble-makers saw his protection qualities stroke services wanted by a host of landlords and business owners across Merseyside.

On my placement to man the front door of the establishment, the realisation dawned on me that this was an opportunity to capitalise on the demand for late-night drinking the club offered that was not getting exploited by the previous front of house.

With my other co-workers, we outlined our conditions of entry: production of a valid membership card, if one couldn't be produced, £3 had to been forfeited into our waiting palms, with no affiliate of the squash club to ever see what was happening downstairs at the entrance, it soon became our little gold mine.

With the previous operators of the entrance being on friendly terms with most of the members, producing a members' card was not the norm on arrival, this soon changed.

We strictly implemented our entrance policy, with desperate drinkers, members and now non-members seeking a continuation of their alcohol consumption on the premises, which they were only too willing in most situations to hand over the admission entrance or the subsequent fine to members not having their membership card with them.

A few months passed by, with the added non-member policy we had introduced, the place was rammed, with a happy management upstairs with the amount of alcohol being sold, coupled with the supplementation of a meagre cut of the door takings, a lot more might I add than what was previously submitted by the previous staff, a lucrative period of hustling prevailed on the steps of the Squashy.

So lucrative was the haul of nuggets to fill our coin purses on these Friday and Saturday evenings, that the furnishings of my new home I had just moved into was courtesy of the entrance fee, so was my new trusty steed, a second-hand purchase of a more prestigious marquee of vehicle became my new mobile, four-wheeled bullion vault, that at the end of each evening's hustle, had its ash tray, glove compartments and side doors brimmed with the subsequent evening's catch.

On one of the nights during our work hours, the chief guardian of our place of resident would show up, Kevin, if not on a passing night out, he would just turn up for a quick oversight of his interest, but more to the point to pick up his family's takeaway meal from the Greek restaurant on the corner of the block, where he also had an overseeing eye of business of protection in.

On this particular night in question, he was on a stop-off visit after a meeting with business associates, which analysing his demeanour, was not just about ingesting plans of concerning interests, but of having the odd glass or two of grandma's homemade moonshine.

Kevin, let's say under an alcoholic influence, was a hard ship to steady to say the least. After a taxation demand by him to us on the front door, which we gave him gladly, the sheriff of Crosby proceeded up the stairs to the members' bar.

The presence of Mad Dog, which was a mantle he went by in the criminal underworld, made for a very uneasy atmosphere in any whereabouts he wandered into.

Unfortunately, the hapless figure of an innocent member and avid squash player sitting at the end of the bar would have Kevin's attention focused on him, or should I say the contents of his shopping bags, which the member had brought inside with him after his visit to Sainsbury's which was just located over the road.

The very well-spoken gentleman's now more slurred speech, whose decision to pop in for a quiet drink, that turned into a little longer than his previous intentions, was probably a bad one, especially for the kippers nestled in the white plastic bag that was no doubt supposed to be an evening meal or morning treat for him and his wife.

A barmaid had come to the top of the stairs and grabbed my attention, to put me in the picture about the gathering momentum of Kevin's antics.

As I gazed through the wire infused glass of the door to where the mischievous Mr Maguire was anchored at the bar, the dejected and solemn figure of one man and his groceries impaired my vision of the intended attention of my scrutiny.

One elbow on the bar, hand cupping his chin, suspending his now surrendering face of helplessness, as a rummaging Mad Dog buried his paws into his proposed week's larder provisions.

Now ripped open exposing the once briny, now smoked ocean dwellers, the fish wielding thug slapped the poor bar prop, pardon the pun, straight across the kipper with the delicacy.

A crusty French baguette now had the scrutiny of the pilfering shopping bag lifter, now bend in half, vaguely resembling a boomerang, it was precisely launched towards the makeshift dance floor as if it was the pride and joy of an aborigine chieftain, but not with the returning behaviour of the Australian outback weapon, striking a somewhat startled occupant of the dance floor on the back.

The victim of the long French missile decided not to retaliate, nothing to do with the Treaty of Versailles, but how they would have been treated by the launcher of the projectile, Kevin, as it was now just kicked to one side and ignored.

The culinary bombardment didn't stop there for the now bewildered parttime ravers. A group of about half a dozen of mixed sex party goers, obviously part of the non-members sect, had definitely participated in a bite of a disco biscuit (Ecstasy) considering the gentle and loving demeanour on having the contents of aisles 2, 6 and 7 of Sainsbury's thrown at them.

With shapes performed more at home in a warehouse with smoke machines and strobe lights than that of a posh members club, which the only smoke it saw was from a thick expensive Havana cigar.

Now with a frisbee-like throw from the origin of the aerial assault, Kevin, with the speed of an American Civil War Gatling gun, was pulverising the happy gang of '90s hippies with Jaffa Cakes.

This in turn encouraged a full-out riotous act of carnage with the soft orange sponge chocolate layered snack, as the Happy Mondays lookalikes rebelled against the rude intrusion, no Jaffa Cake escaped unharmed from this barbaric act of mayhem as they returned fire, casualties rose as a frozen fish finger grazed the forehead of one of the disgruntled gurning ravers.

The Jaffa Cake uprising didn't go down too well with the superpower who started the hostilities, as he now was lining up plates to be thrown in the same frisbee manner, this was my cue to intervene.

A diffusion of the tensions came not really from myself but the timely intervention of a Greek takeaway meal that was ready for pick-up for the shopping bag slinger.

A farcically funny shift when looked back at now, the next shift I will document resides at the other end of the scale, the down-right heinous.

The night now in question under the spotlight, started on the 23rd December 1994, going into the festive Christmas Eve of that year. An all-nighter was the intended advertised duration of the club's hours that evening; this was before the extended hours of business that most night spots call normal these days, was law.

Again, to tell it accurately, let me set the scene: a typical late December evening's weather, not snow but a constant drizzle of rain presented itself over the Dock Road, Liverpool. At that point in time, it was not in the rejuvenated state it resides in today, with a limited amount of light due to the lack of street lamps, the old towering warehouses – a section of one would be my new residence on the payroll as a doorman again – in a fairly now well-established hardcore dance venue called the Hard Dock.

Going back in time to the vibrant hustle and bustle of its heyday, the warehouse was used to store tobacco, shipped from the Americas, with its first resting point being the docks of Liverpool.

The tobacco warehouses built at the very start of the twentieth century. A misinformed or should I say good story-telling caretaker of the then rundown complex, told tales of Liverpool's sinister past regarding the warehouses' involvement in the Transatlantic Slave Trade.

The inaccurate stories that the human cargo, an export from Africa destined for North America, the slaves themselves had been held in the lower sanctums of the cobbled floored buildings, sounded at the time to myself believable, except the story-teller's timeline was somewhat 150 years out.

Liverpool slave ships setting off from the Mersey River Basin carried only exchangeable goods to Africa. On their arrival off the coast of West Africa, they were then filled with the exchanged human cargo then completed the despicable triangular route to the Americas.

During a quite night of business one particular evening, the on-site caretaker gave me a guided tour of the lower reaches of the tobacco-holding buildings where his made-up stories of the captured African slaves were kept.

Still, this impromptu tour coupled with the factual involvement of Liverpool's history in both the cotton and despicable slave trade, it was one of the most unsettling moments I have spent in any building even though the tales being relayed to me were historically muddled. In the pitch black surroundings, with a flimsy hand-held torch as our guide, we navigated our way through the bone-chilling cold bottom rung of the warehouse in an eerie silence.

It didn't stop my imagination conjuring up senses, even a presence, an overwhelming sadness, a sense of paralysing fear embodied me and my guide, which he commented was the reason he never ventured to these parts of his workplace; I totally understood.

Just trying to imagine, to understand the suffering, the detachment, the displacement not just from their homeland but surely from themselves mentally, even though my little excursion wasn't historically correct, it still gave me a sense of the shameful connection Liverpool had with the Transatlantic Slave Trade.

I write about mental illness through trauma, but to really comprehend this atrocity, I tried to grasp it by putting myself lying on the cold wet stone floor that was beneath me, in rags and heavily chained, as the darkness drowned out any light that would have aided my optical nerve into a sense of purpose.

Stomach empty, mouth dry, very likely to have been feverish or diseased. Though the slaves were not stored in these warehouses, their fate was even worse; transported in the holds of ships from their homeland across the turbulent Atlantic is even more unthinkable.

How could it have been possible for these inflicted souls to survive in a psychological sense, never mind the physical, even with their journey or should I say a nightmare hellish existence, only really just starting.

The nightmare hellish situation that would present itself to myself this December evening would pale into insignificance compared to what the poor innocent souls had to endure 250 years previously on route from Africa to the Americas.

But not for one young man, the evening I am focused on turned out to be his last.

Hardcore dance enthusiasts drifted steadily up the wrought iron stairway to the entrance to the club, as if seduced by the distant thump of the base travelling into the ear canal to blast the beat on the awaiting ear drum.

Searchers were compulsory, everyone had no choice, we had the right to refuse admission to any non-compliant objection-opinionated raver.

Past searchers on other themed nights at the venue had produced a loaded high calibre revolver, which the bearer calmly claimed he forgot that he had it upon his person, so as a softener, threw out a compromise that he would take out the shells of the spinning barrelled hand gun, that would have probably stopped a two tonne moose dead in its tracks, never mind a spaced-out pill-popping gurning fun maker.

His compromise of entry was quickly reviewed and even quicker, reneged by me and my associate conducting the frisking.

Back to the evening in question, the time rolled steadily into Christmas Eve. The now filling of the drum and bass emporium embraced its occupants with sounds of the said genre of music. I myself was positioned at the helm of the club to undertake my duties of searching, when a frequent regular of the club walked smiling up the stairs.

This pleasant young man I had on previous visits struck up conversations with. His relaxed pleasant nature made him a person I remembered fondly from the times he had spent on the premises before.

The Bob Marley fan, I presumed because of the tee shirts he had worn in the past, coupled with his Rastafarian appearance, suited his laid-back happy persona.

I started the obligatory search upon him, with an only too willing attitude from the intended scrutinised individual. My actions were strict and adhered to our policies of a stringent clothing and body search. No illegal contraband and certainly no weapon was on this individual, on this night, period.

A host of acclaimed DJs had time slots to spin their particular choices of vinyl during the night, usually turning up just prior to their intended performance.

Into the early hours of the morning, Christmas Eve, one of the allotted DJs and his posse of vinyl box holders clanged their way up the steel-stepped hill to the entrance.

This regular disc spinner was known by us all at the front of house so him and his faithful entourage were ushered in without the pat down and frisking in the manner of what the clientele had to go through when coming up the same ascent.

This by-pass of security was used by one of the DJ's helpers, a good Samaritan in fact, not actually known to the DJ or his party, but a helping hand heading towards the rigorous security checks.

This was an opportunity for this individual to slip in under the cloak of invisibility; what he did actually have under this cloak, the mild-mannered, happy clubber from my earlier search and chat would become the victim of.

Scanning over the crowd, stood at my usual vantage point, the yuletide waves of bobbing craniums were driven by the ensemble of electronic beats, vinyl scratching, with the accompanied vocal interpretation to the mix by the resident MC.

A swift parting of clubbers followed by the running of a person heading straight towards the exit, rose my suspicions that this eager leaver had been involved or trying to avoid something that warranted his urgent exit.

In pursuit, clutching his chest, was my mild-mannered club associate who was the subject of just one of my many searchers that night.

As I followed the two exit-seeking individuals, the latter was shouting some disturbing words, "Stop him, he has just stabbed me, stop him!"

Now on the landing, watching my other work associates take chase of the reported offender, I went to the assistance of the stricken clubber. He held his chest exactly where his heart was beating furiously. Blood seeped through his fingers, of his own handmade dam, that quite evidently could not cope with the flooding of his own blood.

The law required in such an all-nighter to have the presence of a qualified paramedic on duty, who was just so standing in the vicinity at the time and got to work on the stab victim straight away. We laid down the injured person, with the words of the trained medic reiterating, "He is going into shock, he is going into shock!"

I now held the head of the victim, the glowing colour and smile I associated this person with, was now draining away, and was replaced with a scared, panicked bewilderment.

Instructed by the paramedic now to go and get his bag of life-saving implements out of the staff room, I ran barging past happy clubbers having the time of their lives. Little did they know one clubber was in a fight to save his life yards away.

Returning back to the scene, the medic rummaged around his official green holdall producing a pipe-like apparatus, which he promptly tried to insert into the mouth of the victim. Again holding the victim I shouted out encouragement, "Hold on, hold on, stay awake, you can do it, come on, mate, please stay awake!" as he tried to pull the now inserted air wave instrument from his mouth.

"Ambulance, quick, quick!" the medic instructed in a desperate tone to his urgent calling.

"There's one on the way," came the reply over the heads of the growing persons gathering around the immediate area.

The ambulance response was quick, so was the call to the police as my brave co-workers downstairs on the cobbles had prevented the attacker from escape, in a lunging trip from my boss at the time and a desperate struggle to apprehend him, he had the antagonist pinned to the wet gloss shiny cobbled floor of the old warehousing complex.

What we now realised was that we were dealing with a major trauma caused by a large knife. We tried to stem the loss of blood with a couple of pairs of hands and bandages pressing hard on the injury.

With an urgency applied to the pace of the ambulance crew, they hurled themselves up the steel stairs making a louder, peppered clanging as their work shoe apparel struck each step with definite purpose.

In a flash, they had assessed the urgency of this life and death situation, in a rapid response the ambulance personnel jumped down the stairs, missing steps so they could recover a stretcher from their mode of transport quicker.

Still comforting the victim with words of encouragement, I held onto him as he grasped my hand. Myself, the crew of the ambulance and the on-duty medic placed him on the stretcher as we guided our intension, with a gentle, careful descent down the slippery steel stairs.

Our delicate transporting of the victim finished as we loaded him into the awaiting life-supporting form of transport. As the doors were about to close for the frantic journey ahead, I touched the young happy smiling person as I knew him as, reassuring him he would be ok as he struggled frantically to pull the oxygen mask off his face. The doors closed and in a blur of blue lights, the ambulance sped off.

Myself and the paramedic headed back upstairs. A quite bewildered atmosphere had engulfed us both. 40 minutes later, our tired and mentally drained states would become one of shock as well.

Police had arrived and we were given the tragic news that the young man that we had tried so hard to sustain the life of, had been in vain, as he was pronounced dead on his arrival to hospital.

The club now was a murder scene. Blue tape started to get peeled around prominent parts of the bar, a significant area of the pending investigation.

My thoughts drifted to the family of the victim. It was Christmas Eve, they were going to wake up to the news that their loved one had been killed, murdered. With my own investigative thoughts on why did this happen, no sense could I fathom out a conclusion. I was a young father myself, to put myself in the position of the victim's parents, family and friends was just unthinkable to me.

I left the club with the police confirming I would be called in to give a statement at some later date. My mind kept producing the picture in front me of the moment before the doors of the ambulance shut. The whole of this Christmas period I could not erase the vivid playback no matter hard I tried to eradicate it from my thoughts.

I was in a complete daze. I felt disjointed and distant, consumed by my thoughts, accepting this was normal straight after a traumatic incident.

I quietly stored the event of the night into my immediate thoughts for some time afterwards, still trying to remotely untangle the knotted ball of string of reasoning to the timeline in question on the dockland warehouse site.

Contacted now by the police days later, I attended the police station and gave my account of the incident in the way it happened on the night accurately and truthfully. The investigating officers thought I was quite a pivotal witness. On reflection of what the accused had said in his defence, I wouldn't find out what the accused's accounts of the evening were until I was in the witness box giving evidence.

The trial got underway later in the new year. The barrister of the said accused tore into me, undermining my searching practice on the evening in question. More importantly, his client was stating it was the deceased who had smuggled the weapon into the club not him, thus taking it off him, using it in self-defence.

On hearing this absurd suggestion, it dawned on me that they were implying I had not searched the victim sufficiently enough. It was my inadequacy at the front door that led to this situation the court was in session for that day.

The belittlement in front of a packed court room was hard to take and accept, so I fought back in the corner of the dead man, firing back at the defence barrister. Under no circumstances a knife as big as the one that had caused the fatal wound, could have been concealed on the deceased person without me detecting it in the manner of the search I had performed.

With this, he rocked back and forwards with a smug grin on his face, turning his head slightly to the appointed jury, implying silently that my evidence carried no weight for the prosecution.

Leaving the dock, I could not ingest the experience that I had just willing let myself in for. As I headed out of the court room in the public gallery, family and friends of the dead man thanked me, with comments of "well done, you done good."

At that moment, I realised I had tried my utmost to defend the honour of a man who never had the chance to.

On conclusion to the trial, the jury gave a verdict of not guilty of murder, but guilty to the charge of manslaughter, a verdict to this day I just still can't come to terms with.

The jury believed the defence, that the knife went undetected at the front of house by me, concealed on the victim, in turn his own weapon was the course of death, used in self-defence by the accused.

It was a hard pill to swallow. My integrity, my word in a court of law was just dismissed, and this added more negative notions now to my already weak mental stance on the whole incident.

I was offered counselling by the boss of my security firm, I thanked him but declined the offer.

Knife encounters would pop their ugly presence up around this period of time, too frequently than I would care to mention. Again another murder of a friend of only 17 years of age would test my sensitive mental personality, after seeing the young innocent victim lying in wake at his home before his funeral, disbelief, shockingly cruel and unjust, the killer again was never brought to justice.

Friends on nights out or working on the pubs and clubs around Liverpool, would wear jagged slices, carved into their flesh, the end product of their encounters with a sharp piece of Sheffield Steel, near misses that so easily could've ended their lives as well.

Chapter Nine
Self Prescription, Distorted Perception

The mid-nineties generally saw rare and few appearances of Arobieke. If he was spotted, it was never now his intention to bother me. There was no doubt I had outgrown his genre of a typical victim, coupled with the stand I put against him in the decade before, not forgetting the warnings off the Merseyside Police as well, which brings me to a tale of one early hours' routine stop and search by the said boys in blue in the earlier part of the nineties.

After leaving a very well-known rave nightspot in the Bootle area of Liverpool called Quadrant Park in the early hours, ushered to pull over by the signal of blue lights on top of the patrol car behind me, I was asked to step out of my car by the two officers who disembarked from the small Ford Fiesta patrol car.

On doing what they requested of me, they then instructed for me to open the boot of my car. This would've posed a slight problem to any other motorist, but not fortunately for me, considering what the officer would uncover. On me going to the rear of the car to perform the instructed request, one of the officers recognised me because of the notoriety between me and Arobieke.

After the hot, sweaty conditions of the packed shrine dedicated to the abbreviated, once marriage counselling subscribed MDMA, two bare chested rave contraband supplemented stowaways had huddled into the trunk space of my ever-faithful Ford Cortina.

On its creaky opening, exposing it by the beam of light from a police torch, the two occupants imitated scurrying woodlice being uncovered from a piece of woodland debris. The two slightly wired shall I say stowaways failed miserably in their attempt to avoid detection. This actually on first glance looked like they had been bungled into the boot, likened to a Camorra gang's kidnap plot.

In a hurried explanation backed up by the two chattering toothed foetus positioned stowaways that had been substituted against a spare wheel and tin of Castrol GTX, the normal accepted inhabitants of a 1984 GL Ford Cortina, the explanation was accepted.

With a somewhat bewildered look and surprise to his findings, the investigating constable notified me that his accompanying friend and colleague had accusations made against him to the police authority, allegations of racial harassment from Arobieke.

With this connection to the muscle squeezing giant, with a shake of his head, in sync with a little chuckle, "Go on, Mark, mind how you go."

A walkover was granted, the lid was closed on the cowering cargo of the trunk, and off we went, with a wiping of my brow in the process.

Problematic bouts of lows again to my mood would surface every so often after the troubling events of the last ten years, some of them I associated with the saga with Arobieke, repeated visions of my distressed family during the attack on our home, the undeniable hatred of the person created a worry to myself that I would do something in retaliation that I might seriously regret.

The disturbing visions of the fateful night on the old tobacco warehouse site, would still play clear as day in my head, feelings of none worth and some what a guilt after the condemnation of the barrister in the trial plagued me, to some extent I started creating a blame complex upon myself even though it was not warranted.

One particular friend used to lend an ear to listen to my ongoing struggles. It was my companion on my first ever holiday abroad, Rob Bungie Blundell. Always concerned on the times when he knew I was struggling, he would invite me around to either his girlfriend's house at the time or his own flat after I had finished work at the gym.

The pair of us loved the sport of boxing. A night I won't forget was when we watched Iron Mike Tyson climb through the ropes to fight in Manchester. Our seats near enough ring side was one of those moments when Iron Mike walked past us on his ring walk and hair stood up on the back of my neck.

If not attending the big fights, we would watch them on TV together, when on the really big fight nights we would make it somewhat of an occasion where the drinks would flow and certain other requirements that I thought were needed on such marathon nights.

Having both trained at Kirby ABC for a period of time, in which Rob showed a gift for his punching power, with his good looks, he also grabbed a stand-in part, documenting about the life of boxer Freddie Mills, Rob doubled for the actor playing the boxer in all the fight scenes.

HMP Liverpool would be a showcase for the young boxers of the club one afternoon, with the added bonus for the inmates of the newly crowned World Champion, Kirby native Paul Hoko Hodkinson, to parade his new waist wear, the WBC Featherweight belt around the prison's sports hall.

Like in my previous ring appearance, this time not matched with my brother but with my best mate, again my personality never presented a 'whoever is in front of you, punch there lights out' attitude, I danced around the ring avoiding a tear up, with also the fear of getting belted on the whiskers by Rob's mighty southpaw left hand anaesthetic punch.

Married now and with the added addition of a beautiful little daughter we named Danielle, family life was perfect.

Creeping turbulent weather systems of depression though would for some reason still present a challenge to myself.

I blamed or put it down to the use of anabolic steroids that I had broken the seal of purity with regarding my own drug use.

On such low mood occurrences, I would take up the offer, mainly of a weekend after working on the pubs or clubs. I would venture into the rocky powdered mountains of cocaine at friends' houses. This temporary fix of the self-prescribed Bogotá bullion, dispersed the black rolling clouds of doom and replaced them with smiling rainbows.

Just like the sun catching the falling moisture droplets, causing multi coloured prisms in the sky, it was a very temporary state of mind that was replaced with bolts of lightning in the form of flashbacks of past events and thunderous noises of paranoia, that my super enhanced sense of hearing was amplifying, It was so acute, I swear I could hear the local church mice scurry across the parquet flooring of the local vicarage wearing comfy slippers, due to the stimulant that had been vacuumed up by my nasal passages.

At this point all forms of any physical exercise took a back seat, as my limited energy supply, due to work and burning the candle at both ends, would be channelled to spending quality time with my young family. With the subsequent inactivity, my depression worsened, so did the weight around my waist.

So one night after work, at around 10.30pm and in the cover of darkness, I set off on what could not have been more than a 15-minute gasping trudge to the bottom of the street and back.

Arriving back at my doorstep, a disgusted, embarrassed analysis took place with myself, but strangely enough, after the plodding exasperated trundle, I felt surprisingly good, lifted in mood, this was good I thought.

So after every late shift in the gym, which was generally three nights a week, under the cloak of darkness, I would slip out into the night to pound the pavements around my home.

With the trio of late evening workouts, it started to abate the frequently occurring bouts of depression. With the now improved running gate coupled with subsequent weight loss, I ventured into the world of the day light jogger. This was quite a running step forward due to my ingrained form of anxious awareness from the years gone by of twitching at the presence of Arobieke.

Even though I had been improving my aerobic capacity during the hours of darkness, I never explored the woodland areas around my home, that I never knew even existed until donning my new best friend, my running shoes.

The experience of a fast-paced ramble through the countryside, bolstered my defences against the debilitating negative thoughts I was accustomed to, a hovering float above the turbulence I once flew straight into, I could say was now a high, euphoria in fact, and I wanted it more and more.

My exploration into the world of the recreational runner had not gone unnoticed by my next-door neighbour, an avid fund raiser for the local community and the British Legion, he would soon make me an offer I could not refuse.

Housed in one of the local primary schools was a learners' swimming pool, erected to aid the villagers' children gain the life-saving skill, after one too many unfortunate drownings in the area. The mission put to me was to help raise the required sum of £70,000 or to at least put a dent in the estimated cost to refurbish the now tired looking pool for it to continue its role as a must part in the local school's curriculum.

My part to play in the proceedings was a big ask considering my inexperience, coupled with my weight more accustomed to that of a shot putter, it was to run in the New York City marathon, 26.2 miles around the five boroughs of the Big Apple.

What an opportunity it was for me to at last go State side, and raise money for a worthwhile cause that my own children would benefit from. I seized the opportunity with a focus I had not had since my days of being a competitive junior muscle mechanic.

I remember this period of time in my life fondly. The preparation for the task ahead brought my appreciation of a balanced and healthy functioning mind, as well the beauty, the exhilaration of running and spending time on woodland trails, seeing the change of seasons in all their glory.

The go ahead to prepare for the event started in the January of 1997, the date of the marathon was at the start of November of the same year, a near on full year of seasonal changes I would witness on the landscape of my running journey.

The biting cold runs of the winter made me feel never more alive. Preferred trails would be ones in the heart of the woods not ventured by many, the only evidence of company was when blankets of snow would cover the ground exposing deer activity or other smaller woodland occupants.

My now self-made pounding footprints in the soft ground had created my own personal running track. The emergence of spring would bring the emergence of seas of blue from the perennial visitor, the bluebell. Clusters of daffodils stood tall as if looking over the shoulders of their smaller counterparts. The fresh changing colours and smells breathed life into the wood and to myself.

The vastly covered summer fields of yellow rapeseed flowering put me in my own wonderful world of Oz. It was as if I had already been granted my wish from the Wizard for a healthier functioning brain as I happily glided past on my regimented runs.

The slight summer breeze moved the bright sea of rolling waves of corn. The same golden waves of a renewed, reinvented cognitive way of thought were now also swaying comfortably together in my head, brushing to one side my once troubled irrational thinking.

Autumns showing signalled I was near my proposed target of engagement in the Big Apple, a vivid reliable memory of comfort I still use today as a coping strategy when in times of need. When a few days away from my departure, I took my two young children into the woods which I called my own little Eden.

In their Wellington boots, they happily kicked the fallen leaves of the year's treetop foliage, splashing in the streams I had splashed through myself in the summer, that gave a cool escape from the heat of the day's workout.

I showed them the solidified footprints of my efforts in the ground that once was mud in the winter months, as I navigated my way around the unstable water-logged earth; the evidence of my presence would soon be taken by the wood and lost forever under the cascading leaves and inevitable rains.

Looking back, I think I was subconsciously saying thank you to the wood for my rehabilitation, just like I would've to a doctor or other medical professional for their expert services.

With the punishing regime of training, numerous shorter distant practice races, I was ready for my tilt of running 26.2 at a pace through the streets, parks and boroughs of the famed US city. My efforts on the trails and tarmac had melted away nearly 5 stone of surplus body weight; just as significant, the weight of depressive states had also been cast into their relevant waste disposal bin.

As the iron bird dropped into JFK, the first point of reference that New York City was on the horizon, an unflattering cloud of black smog that hovered over the city, but on this day, this beautiful sunny day in my head, there was no smog obscuring the skyscrapers of my mind, the sky was the limit for my cleansed mind, body and soul.

My NYC adventure would be undertaken on my own, but my sponsors had booked through a sports tour company, which brought about a rooming situation with a complete stranger. It turned out a university graduate from Watford would be my base companion, a gamble of compatibility, yes, but as it turned out, it was fine.

Race day was on a Sunday, so Friday was a sightseeing gathering with all the other runners the sports touring business had accumulated from the UK.

I personally decided to hit the iconic streets in a lonesome quest of enlightenment, the same avenues and buildings made famous in my favourite films like *Ghostbusters*, *Home Alone 2*, where one of my non-sporting idols uprooted to and ultimately met his demise, John Winston Lennon, to absorb the sights, the smells of a place I had only dreamed of visiting less than 12 months previously.

My solo effort of touring this concrete jungle, was one I would never forget, but would also carry a tinge of embarrassment, in that it still makes me cringe to this day on the realisation of what my own sightseeing skills stroke instincts led me to.

As an Englishman in New York, the lyrics of Sting resonated in my head as I strolled the sidewalks and avenues. A human outline had surrounded one of the many towering superbly architected buildings, thus drawing my attention to it.

Due to the eager people starting to mass in the queue, I calculated that this was a place of high interest to the public, so without further ado, I joined the long line that made up the chain on my self-imposed tour of the Big Apple.

Dressed in my neat branded track suit and trainers, I certainly looked the part of a pre-event athlete, maybe stood out slightly amongst my fellow in line associates, all of whom showed an anxious, cold and weathered disposition to get to the entrance of whatever this gallery, museum or other place of interest had to offer, which was situated around the corner, out of sight from me and the stragglers at the back.

After a while, patiently shuffling slowly forward in line, I noticed on the distant horizon of the sidewalk the approaching band of runners from the UK that I had flew over with on the same sports package trip, including my new roommate.

The group notably stood out due to the flag on a pole held aloft by the appointed guardian shepherd guide. The visual aid was for any separated stray sheep of the flock to reattach themselves to the group, thus not leaving them to the mercy of the wolves of New York.

The detection that I brought to myself was swift by the posse of 'I Love New York' t-shirt wearing brigade of tourists, with their slow intentional walk-by, forced due to the congestive state of the side walk, with it came shaking of heads, coupled with looks of disgust.

One under-the-breath comment didn't escape the attempt to evade my listening devices, "Typical Scouser, of all the bare-faced cheek, what will he try next, steal the hub caps of a yellow cab?"

Why did I warrant such bitterness? The sheer distaste in their faces could've turned me into stone, just like the structure I was hugging trying to enter. After all, all I was trying to do was self-educate myself with the exhibitions, the art galleries and any more places of interest that would broaden my general knowledge of this world-renowned unique metropolis.

I certainly did broaden my knowledge on turning the corner, exposing me to what I was actually stood in line for.

The only knowledge I gained that day was simple, to be like a sheep and follow a shepherd in the big expanses of an unfamiliar concrete jungle.

To my shock and embarrassment, the 50-minute wait in the queue of oddly dressed, weathered faced personnel was not for one of the acclaimed tourist attractions, but it was to receive a daily dose of nourishment of soup, from the volunteers working on behalf of one of the city's soup kitchens for the destitute and homeless.

After a deliberately reluctant slow passing of a paper bowl, and an additional look from head to toe of non-acceptance in my quest for a bowl of the Bronx broth by the half-willing volunteer, whose thinking obviously created a suspicion due my immaculately dressed appearance that I was after a free meal, courtesy of the city of New York.

I shuffled down the conveyer belt of charitable helpers in my gleaming new sneakers, too lost for words to explain my predicament that I was lost in New York's normal tourism itinerary.

The condition of the footwear of the other soup receivers showed wear and tear of their constant years of use trekking around the paved streets of the city, just like the tread of a bald car tyre in some instances had blown out, exposing the frozen feet of the wearer.

With a splashing dunk of the huge ladle into the mother bowl, its contents were then emptied into my disposable soup holder. At this point now, I just wanted one of the steaming grids from the subway to just open up and swallow me into the abyss.

A sincere thank you of acknowledgement for their hard work for such a good course, I turned meekly away with the eyes of all the volunteers burning into the back of my head.

The outcome of my misadventure was the best dining I sampled during my entire stay in New York, the cuisine itself I likened it to my home city's own delicacy, scouse.

The other understanding brought out of my experience standing in line with some of the most deprived people of New York, which I have also come to recognise on the other occasions I have walked and ran the streets of the Big Apple, are the amount of severely unwell people suffering with mental health issues.

From war veterans to people who had fell on hard times through unemployment, their written explanations on pieces of cardboard, highlighting their predicaments, their mannerisms gave away their mental health insecurities, as they sat begging and wandering around aimlessly on one the most opulent zip codes stroke shopping thoroughfares in the world, 5th Avenue.

A disturbing memory I have whilst I was walking down 5th Avenue accompanied by my young daughter on another separate holiday across the pond, the same avenue where the famed Trump Tower is situated, the jewellers Tiffany's and other marquee retailers, where the abundance of wealth was personified by them all, was the lone bare-footed figure of an African American, yes, the poor soul was bare-footed, feet ravaged, deformed and bleeding, talking out loud to the only person willing to listen to his distorted words of thinking, himself.

Another time while sat on a bench outside The Plaza Hotel with my son and his friend watching, the comings and goings of the *Brewster's Millions* and *Home Alone 2* centre piece, lying on the bench next to us, awoken by the noise of the hustle and bustle of the busy vicinity, was a middle-aged Caucasian women neatly dressed and kept, her mind though was far from being in order and kept in the same way as her appearance, she arose from her slumber with cries like that of a Banshee followed by a host of non-descript obscenities, a result of the detachment from reality and I suppose society.

Two stark contrasts to what you would've expected to see around the plush surroundings of Manhattan. On both occasions witnessing this, a hospital bed would have been more suitable than a sidewalk for both. More shocking was the avoidance, the non-pity, the blatant cloak of invisibility the surrounding public and law enforcement threw over these walking wounded of the mind; it was really quite shocking.

Yes, I have gone off in a tangent, but the sheer divide is plain to see in the US. If you can't afford health care, the acceptance of hospitalising conditions walking around in plain view is an attitude of so be it.

We have a lot to be thankful for in our great NHS, such visual mental abnormalities would have succumbed to some sort of intervention and dealt with, in most cases any way.

When I did actually re-route my built-in sat nav to direct me to the accepted tourist destinations, I wasn't to be disappointed, especially one building that I had the fortune to have a rooftop walk on. It was the South Tower of the World Trade Centre.

A chilling comment I made to another rooftop rambler, was on seeing how close aeroplanes flew to the iconic buildings. My analysis was that it wouldn't take much for one of the by-passing passenger jets to veer of course and to collide with the two sky scraping structures.

Of course history now tells the horrors of 9/11. Since my first visit, I have gone back to the site on numerous occasions to pay my respects, to gradually see the rise again of not just another iconic building but the rise of the people of the great city against overwhelming odds and adversity, a truly inspiring example of the power of the human mind.

As for the marathon, it would test my own mental fortitude to the limit. The worst rain seen on the annual race day ever, added to the elation of just completing the gruelling course in a respectable time of 3 hours 43 minute. As for the regime, the shedding of 5 surplus stone, the taming of my demons that dwelled inside me, with the object of raising a substantial amount of money towards the renovation of the children's swimming pool also fulfilled, with the boost to my own mental dexterity huge as well, my mission was a success.

The next year brought another opportunity, this time a business one. The once health club that I joined as a child in 1983, that gave me my first job in '86 till that present moment, would become my own enterprise, the ownership of the gym itself.

Within a business partnership, we set out to give the gym a new lease of life coupled with the enthusiasm of new ownership it badly needed. We reopened on the 25th March 1998 with a renewed surge of membership. It looked like the jump into self-employment was a good one.

Just over six months into my now-flourishing rejuvenated business venture, the event that changed the lives of many would take place in the gym I had spent most of my life growing up in. The date was 1st October 1998, a day still so vividly ingrained in my memory and senses that if nudged, encouraged by a systematic trigger, would catapult me back in time to relive it over and over again.

Chapter Ten
The Murder Gym

The Autumn day presented a clear blue sunny sky, with a crispness in the air on my usual Thursday morning in my duty of opening up the gym.

A note of commodities was written down by myself of what was needed for our pre- or post-workout protein shake specialities from the local supermarket. With the arrival of my business partner, I left the gym supervised, as I went about my errands.

On my return, the gym was busy with its regulars going through their usual exercise regimes, the thuds of heavy dumbbells hitting the thick rubber flooring, Olympic plates slamming together as weight increased on bars and machines, the encouraging comments of push, one more rep, easy, the suited returning moans of effort coming back as the lifts and movements were undertook.

In the midst of the morning regulars, there was one unfamiliar face, a non-member or a new subscribed member unknown to me as I scanned the gym to say my good mornings.

I checked the till receipt to see if this stranger had joined our family-ran business which now included a very popular Kids' Club I held on a Saturday afternoon – this particular day I was going to bring my pre-school 3-year-old daughter to work with me, but a change of plan at the last minute on leaving for work, fate took that visit out of my hands.

The stranger that I myself had not seen before, had not joined the ranks but had paid for a non-members session, but apparently had trained a few times earlier on in the week.

As 11.30am approached, the quiet individual had performed his not so punishing, methodical workout. On retrieving his holdall from the changing room, he proceeded to pass by the reception stroke refreshment area that was in the centre of the gym and was where I was standing behind.

A good bye and thank you was attempted by myself – trying to engage in a conversation might've resulted in a new fully subscribed member – zero acknowledgment, just a cold fixed stare towards his attended path was the uncomfortable return to my gestures.

Sitting down on a flat exercise bench, literally about ten feet or so away from my position behind the counter, ten or so feet further was the exit/entrance to the gym, his holdall now in between his legs, was where the frosty cold stranger decided to perch himself.

Facing him, doing the last repetitions of his chosen exercise, was my friend and occasional security boss, Kevin Maguire. Next to him his common law wife, Linda. To the right, feet away from the seated non-member, was a young man, a new close associate of Kevin's and a friend of mine, Nathan Jones.

What happened in the next moments that I will now document, is still hard for me to recall, but at the same time is so crystal clear, that over two decades later, they play in the finest clarity in my mind and always will.

Over the speakers of the gym admitting the requested workout music of the morning, a CD had been stuck repeating the same track over and over again. I knelt down from my position to remedy the situation.

On rising from behind the reception where the music system was situated, the subsequent non-member launched himself into a shooting stance, aiming the barrel of a hand gun firing at Nathan Jones then turning his fixed deliberate aim attention, firing at Kevin Maguire.

Nathan stood up from his piece of apparatus and headed to the back of the gym, to the changing rooms. The gun spewed out the rest of its arsenal towards Kevin, one bullet missing, ricocheting of the metal dumbbells and exploding into pieces.

The other projectile hit its intended target quite easily considering the distance from which it was fired. I stood motionless, witnessing the bullet rip through Kevin's body, the ensuing injuries forcing blood to emit heavily from the victim's mouth, muffling the words of reaction from Kevin, "OW, OW!"

A heroic leap of defence to become a human shield by Linda, his life-long companion and mother to his four children, rendered the situation that presented itself to me incomprehensible to digest by my own mental capacity at the time.

Frozen for the split seconds of the calculated carnage, I soon realised the severity of the situation as the gun man retreated, still brandishing the weapon in my direction before putting it back into the holdall that hid the sinister contents before its use.

I ducked down for cover, looking out from behind the side of my reception to witness the escape. With what still seemed his ice-cold unruffled manner, he quite steadily but with haste made his exit from the scene of the crime.

A feeling of déjà vu and disbelief after my other experience years before suffocated me. As I went over to help Kevin on his back cradled by his loving partner, we put him on his side so he wouldn't choke on the heavy flow of his own blood.

The desperate situation never went unnoticed by a passing off-duty fireman who joined us on our life saving attempt. Instructions again were given to me by an expertly trained first aider, as mouth to mouth was performed by the good Samaritan, I performed the chest compressions on command.

A severed obstruction from the air waves of the victim, the result of the bullet criss-crossing around the inside of the torso was expelled, spitting it out through his efforts of mouth to mouth by the off-duty fire fighter, at the same time trying to control his instinctive gagging reflex reaction to the horror in which he had been confronted with.

Realising now it was a hopeless task with our limited skills, we needed urgent medical equipment and personnel fast. I rang 999 for help.

The serious crime squad later said of the call that I made to the emergency services, was one of the most harrowing calls they had ever had to listen to in their investigating of such cries for help.

After my frantic conversation with the superbly trained diligent 999 call operator, I headed into the changing rooms to where Nathan ran for cover. There outstretched on the floor, again like his friend, blood was gurgling from his mouth. I positioned him on his side as I frantically looked for a bullet hole.

The lifting up of Nathan's t-shirt revealed the horrific injury. The near enough point blank aim had hit to the left side of his chest, directly positioned in line where his beating heart would've been.

Looking for the exit wound, I looked at his back. With no visible signs, I knew the bullet never exited the heavily muscled individual. I hoped it had been lodged in the pectoral muscle fibres before it could've burrowed its way to the blood pumping muscle, the heart.

The first response personnel to enter the gym were the ones of the armed variety. Two burly armed response officers with sub machine guns entered to secure the building, to secure the safety of the paramedic crew, to make certain they were in no danger before they attended to the victims.

Keeling down now with Kevin, Linda still holding him in her arms, the paramedic crew took over. On their attendance to Kevin, I queried who was going to attend to the other shooting victim, his reply was one of surprise.

"There's been two shot?" he queried, puzzled.

Myself and Linda retreated to the reception counter top. The woman was small in height, but if measured in the size of her bravery and devotion, the measuring tape would soar above in its enormity to any earthly mountain range.

What she had exhibited by putting herself right into the firing line, throwing herself on top of her partner, using her own body to protect the integral part of her family unit, is a part of this heinous event that I remember with an overwhelming amount of admiration and pride.

The calm, composed woman still vocally reciting prayers, asked if I could phone the vicar of her local church, in which she was an active parishioner. A man of the cloth would be an added human presence of strength, an underpinning of stability and reassurance, at a time of unconceivable testing of faith.

The two medics performed their vital observations on Kevin, then with a slow walk, one of the life savers, trying to assemble, rehearsed the forthcoming appropriate wordings of speech, exhibiting the body language of one carrying the burden of news so dreaded, delivered the earth-shattering news to Linda.

"We are so sorry, we tried everything possible."

Kevin was pronounced dead at the scene, possibly instantly the paramedic revealed. With this, their attention then switched to the other casualty, Nathan.

Their analysis of Nathan's condition was swift as the louver doors of the men's changing rooms crashed open with the urgent push of the stretcher bearers. I quickly cleared obstructions of gym equipment out the way, as the multi-tasking medics pushed the stretcher at the same time tending to the critically injured occupant of the wheeled bed. Nathan was whisked through the gym and out into the waiting ambulance.

A quiet bewilderment settled amongst the remaining non-emergency and law enforcement personnel left in the gym. A comprehension was sought as to what had just prevailed. The adjustment back to reality I craved, but this was reality, this did happen, this was so very real.

The place was now swarming with police officials, crime investigators, forensics, and outside the inevitable securing of the building with blue tape of a crime scene, kept at bay concerned friends and residents of the area and an ever-growing media presence.

The suited police officials started to take charge of the now murder scene and as things stood at that moment in time, the attempted murder of another, taking into account who had been the hitman's victims, a picture was quickly forming that this was a calculated gangland execution.

After being told that a minibus for the witnesses was on its way to take us to the local police station, I phoned my wife to tell her of the horrific events that had unfolded that morning before the television and radio stations had a chance to broadcast it publicly.

In a dazed state of shock, I relayed the grim news briefly to my wife. The incomprehensible state travelled down the phone line as she struggled with my interpretation of my supposed morning at work.

After placing the receiver of the phone down slowly, again struggling to wake up from this nightmare, hoping to find myself clutching the pillow of my bed on waking, but no my eyes were wide open, no pinch was needed, this was no sleep disturbing figment of my imagination.

The mini bus now waited outside. With this I made my way over to the lifeless body of Kevin, my friend, a son, a brother, father and soul mate to his closest, Linda.

As tough and as hardened a man could possibly be, with a unique personality, whose life had just been cut short in a devastating blink of an eye, with a kiss upon his forehead, I said my goodbye and left the gym.

I also without realising it, was saying goodbye to the gym I once knew, for it wouldn't ever be the same place to me again.

The happy, cherished memories of entering my utopia at 13 years of age, growing up into a young man, shielded from the bad influences, the wrong directed roads of young adolescent associates, now replaced with the murderous scenes of deeply fathomed evil.

Behind the blue tape in front of the crowd that had gathered was my best mate Rob, who was visibly upset, but now with a look of relief on his face knowing it wasn't me who had been a victim of one of the bullets.

"Are you ok, Mark?" he repeated, "Are you ok?"

With just a nod of my head, I gestured yes, as words would've failed me, giving away I wasn't ok, far from it.

We all boarded our appointed multi-seated form of transport and left for the station under the watchful supervision of Merseyside police. This police scrutiny, little did I know would continue not just for our less than the half a mile journey to the appointed police station, but for a long time afterwards into the coming months and year ahead.

On our arrival to the now converted major incident headquarters, we were all systematically interviewed. My time in front of the two detectives started with the devastating news that Nathan, with all the drastic attempts by the paramedics failed in their attempt to keep him alive on the journey to the hospital.

The bullet had actually pierced his heart. It was now a double murder inquiry – a rare double gangland execution.

With my hands now covering my face, I wept for the first time since the event, on the realisation that it was now five young children that would grow up without a father, Kevin's four children and Nathan's infant son.

The subsequent events of the morning according to myself were noted down by the two jotting note pad detectives, early thirties in age, suited with the jackets of the two-piece suit now hung on the back of their chairs, making the task of the long written statement more comfortable to undertake.

As the interview concluded, I was asked to take off my blood-stained clothes. An alternate wardrobe was made available to me, bagged up and labelled in front of me, they were sent off to the forensic team.

With a relaxed attitude and demeanour towards me, after about five hours, the officers said I could leave. I was shown the door and cast out onto the front pavement of the police station.

Alone, my senses of hearing and sight were disorientated. I non-specifically walked away from where I spent most of the day making my official account of the morning in a complete daze. This is what they meant by the term shell shocked, well and truly, I thought to myself.

I headed to the nearest place of refuge I could think of to gather my senses, Rob's flat, my confidante in time of need. My direction now had a purpose, but so did the company that was following me have purpose of direction, to follow my every step, the police.

Reaching my safe haven, I was met by a cluster of friends who had gathered outside at my intended destination, knowing that I might just head to my close friend's sanctuary.

With an outpouring of sympathy from the friends, I asked if one of them could take me to my parents' house nearby. I had not even had the inkling to get word to them I was ok, with my mind totally devoid of any rational train of thought. Hopefully my wife had put them in the picture of what had happened to stop any unnecessary worry earlier on in the day.

Huge sighs of relief greeted me on my arrival at my home where I grew up, even though they knew it was not me who had been shot. My parents and my three brothers had all gathered together as a unit of strength for each other waiting for news from myself. My youngest brother who worked in an office in the city centre at the time, was actually told of my demise wrongly just after the news was filtering out after the shootings, only being corrected not long after the idle gossip of an office busybody got out of control.

My transportation, the journey home to my young family, a complete blur, I can recollect vividly both sides between my homeward journey, but the actual time in the middle, the journey itself lost, my drowning in the thoughts of the past day eradicated the twenty-five minutes of recollection completely.

My consciousness returned as my two young children greeted me with their usual hugs and kisses on their daddy returning home from work. Their daddy in turn squeezed them tight and uncontrollably broke down into floods of tears, of relief, and an appreciation for their lives and that of his next of kin.

'ICE MAN SLAYS GANGLAND BOSSES IN GYM EXECUTION' – bold, big printed headlines displayed on the front page of the local evening newspaper on the night of the murders.

The name given to the hitman was from my statement I gave to the police, as I described his cold demeanour minutes before and during his ordered executions.

The events in the gym had also made the evening news of the national television studios, who relayed the day's goings-on at Crosby Health and Leisure to the nation sitting down to their evening meals.

Chapter Eleven
The Aftermath

For the next three weeks, the police forensics team had charge of the gym. A portable incident room was now situated outside amongst the sea of floral tributes. Members of the gym had to attend the porta cabin at some point, for the reasoning of elimination of their unique stamp of identification, finger prints.

From outside the premises, all that could be seen was the in-and-out activity of forensic personnel covered head to toe in their white non-contamination overalls.

My first night's sleep after the shootings brought replayed visions to my dreams of the whole incident time and time again. No let-up would my mind give me, no respite away from the recurring pictures. The bang of the firearm as it was discharged rang repeatedly in my ears, the horrific effects of the bullets, the ending of life that had played out in front of me was stuck on play and repeat constantly in my disturbed thoughts.

These visions continued on my awakening, there was no let-up from them. As the investigations of the police took their course during the coming days and weeks, I was called into other interviews again to go through the hours pre and post shooting.

On one particular interview, I was put into a relaxed state of mind so I could relive the situation in detail. This was easy, stirring the embers of my smouldering recollections didn't take much, as the ultra-high-definition details of the events were playing constantly in my one-tracked mind of occupying thoughts.

Three weeks had passed now, with no financial support from my once thriving business, due to the confiscation of the building by the police. Financial pressure was now building up, bills needed to be paid at home and in the gym, rent for the building was backing up to a substantial amount of arrears, more importantly, I had young mouths to feed and clothe.

I was told the forensics had concluded their business of in-depth scrutiny, so I was asked to meet detectives inside the gym one afternoon so they could hand me back the keys.

What met my eyes was just too hard to comprehend, nearly making me break down as I pushed the door open.

I wasn't looking at my beloved gym that was my whole life and had been for at least two thirds of it.

The only way I can describe the inside of my business premises that was thrust into my non-believing line of vision, was that of sheer disrespectful vandalism.

The disbelief to the extent of coverage of fingerprint dust was just simply too much to take. From the loft space down to the ground gym floor, it looked like it had been ransacked by a band of marauding pirates desperately looking for some loot to pilfer.

With a dropped jaw of disbelief, I scanned the once colourful gym space, the lead grey coloured fine powder had been completely smothered onto everything inside the entire gym, the walls, the ceiling, every last bit of gym equipment had been desecrated, even the food mixer we made protein shakes with was given the same treatment.

I was heart-broken, only just over 6 months previous I had spent my entire life-savings, with added loans to make my life-long dream come true. It was ruined.

It was like watching a grey and white cine-film reel play live in front of me, no colour exhibited itself to me, just like the now dark cloudy storm system forming in my head of epic proportions.

I held out an unwilling hand of acceptance for the keys off the detective, with the question whose responsibility is it to put this right. The returning worrying reply was, "I will see what I can do for you."

With that, I left the shambolic surroundings behind me, crushing the metal keys in my hand, wanting to just launch them now as far away from me as possible, with the notion of never to return, but this wasn't an option.

I had no time to waste. The next day I set out with the objective to start the clean-up operation until the police sent in their own cleaning team.

These positive objectives would soon disappear on the appearance of four suited detectives not long after I had arrived at the gym, one of which I had not encountered before. These were all part of the serious crime squad.

In a complete change of attitude towards myself, a more intimidating no-niceties approach was being exhibited, that could especially be said about the detective I had not encountered previously, with the fragile tree branch in my head, this out-the-blue tactic, it was just about ready to snap.

I couldn't understand where the line of questioning was going. After all, I was a victim of this atrocity as well, my whole life had been turned upside down, then it dawned on me after the detectives left, I must be under some sort of suspicion. Surely not? How could this be at all possible for them to think of me as an accessory for a double murder plot, but I was, me and my business partner were at the top of the list of suspects.

This ludicrous suggestion prompted me to seek advice of a solicitor. On the appointed lawyer's guidance, speaking to the police would all be done in front of an officiated representative from the solicitor's company from then onwards.

My cooperation prior to the change in tone from the police had been one of only too willing. This added pressure was totally unjust as I balanced on this tight rope, balance pole in hand, now with an itchy nose, a loosening of my grip, a one-handed attempt to relieve that itch, I would've plummeted into a pit of despair.

With the communication from my solicitor landing on the detective's desk, they then made it clear they would have no part financially or any other involvement whatsoever in the restoring of the business back into the functional gym it once was, it would all be left for us to undertake.

The painstaking challenge got underway. This pain was made even more challenging than I could've ever imagined. Minutes into my rolled-up-sleeves clean-up attempt, it abruptly came to a sudden halt.

Thinking the forensic team once finishing their part in the proceedings would've cleaned up, not just the staining fingerprint dust, but the remainder of the actual murder aftermath, oh no, far from it.

Thick pools of now dried solidified blood, pieces of fragmented flesh, spat out by the life-saving attempt from the heroic off-duty fireman, it was now my unforgiving task to clean up my own friend's murderous end.

On my hands and knees, I scraped and scrubbed the aftermath carnage caused by one of the bullets fired. The scrubbing motion from my kneeling down position became more ferocious, as I bit my lip with anger, venting it to the visions in my head to the people I blamed for this moment in time I found myself in. Blood had found its way to the seams of the rubber matting joins, peeling the heavy Matt's up, it revealed a crust layering of blood on the concrete floor below, the transferred remains of my efforts had turned my bucket of water into a chestnut dirty colour. Moving onto the next evident remains of the other fallen victim at the back of the gym, the changing rooms, resuming into a kneeling position again, my fixed stare was on the large pool of solidified blood just within arm's reach away… I froze, just staring down at my proposed intension of cleaning scrutiny, tears began to fall uncontrollably down from my rigid face, on top of the cloud shaped pool of dark crimson red, the fluid from my face in turn woke up the surface making it run now into a less solid form, making the undesirable task even more incomprehensible.

It was yet another added insult to an already debilitating injury list. Whether an intentional or an unintentional move by the police, it was wrong on every level for me to get down on my hands and knees, to scrape and scrub, and rectify the post-killing carnage.

It was a hopeless task of removing the grey fine powder from every nook and cranny, but with our best efforts, we got the gym into some sort of shape to re-open. This would be the acid test of survival for the business. Would people return to the 'Murder Gym', a name given to us by the local Liverpool evening newspaper, or would non-attendance be the straw that broke the camel's back, we were about to find out.

With a police portable incident room still positioned outside, still undertaking the finger printing of every single recent and past member's unique print, it was a constant reminder of what had taken place weeks before.

Strangely enough, the male attendance actually didn't take that much of a hit. The same unfortunately couldn't be said about the women; 90% of them never returned. As for the Saturday's Kids Club, that also took a major dive.

To be fair, I totally understood. Would you have wanted your children attending a club where a double gangland murder execution had took place; I know I wouldn't have let my children attend.

I was just thankful most of the male regulars returned; they knew we were the innocent victims here as well. We even had new clients enrolling, they were very much welcome, but the curiosity of a membership for some enquirers was not their real motive, their conversation quickly turned to where did the shootings happen, where did the gunman shoot from, where did Maguire die, where did Jones run to.

On a few occasions this actually happened, ghoul hunters wanting me to give them a guided tour of the city's new unofficial tourist attraction, biting my tongue, they were asked to leave instantly, in some cases, in not such a business-like manner, more like a disgruntled old codger of a neighbour at the end of his tether with a ball that kept getting kicked into his garden and landing in his prised flower bed of gladioli.

A short time after reopening, the removal of the portable police incident room from outside the gym was a welcome sight.

The constant reminder to passers-by of the fateful episode had gone, so having to pop out the gym for supplies like postage stamps, stationary etc., to the local post office situated two doors away from my business premises, was very convenient and now less intimidating to face, but again a twist of fate would leave me dumbstruck literally days after reopening.

A slight sense of a very normal routine was coming back to me because of this simple little errand to the post office. Unfortunately, this feeling would last very momentarily as I walked, yes, you have guessed it, into another Lemony Snicket event, straight into an armed robbery outside the post office two doors away.

Standing in disbelief, a poor security guard who had just stepped out of his impenetrable mobile bank vault was having his prized secured money holder, which was chained to his arm, bolt-cut off his trembling limb, while a gun was pointed at him to encourage his yelled instructions not to resist.

In a well-orchestrated heist, it was then passed along to two sledge hammer wielding associates on the corner yards away, who then began to smash the hell out of it before the bright dye that was now getting expelled from the once secured black box, could destroy all of the valuable bank of England shiny new notes it was shielding inside.

Once all the ski masked participants had jumped into their getaway car and sped off, I decided to give my returning normality trip to the post office a miss.

This event to the normal Joe public to witness, would have probably caused asterisks; to me, it was one of my now increasing series of unfortunate events.

Brushing it aside as if the event was not serious enough to warrant the deployment of my flight or fight hormones, I returned to my counter of the gym and proceeded to make a milk shake, worryingly composed, considering the happenings on my visit to the neighbouring post office.

Later that day, two CID officers entered the gym, doing their compulsory door-to-door enquires warranted after such a crime, when they asked, "Mark, did you see anything?"

My reply was a resounding, "Nothing, I saw nothing."

One of the detectives then said in an expectant tone to his voice, "I thought you might say that."

Both then turned and left the building, in a you have got enough on your plate type of resolution.

Normality for me mentally now was to deal with the reoccurring visions of the fateful murderous day itself. Having to return to the murder scene near enough everyday was a crushing experience, slowly chipping away at my sanity.

Getting asked continually about the episode, in my own smaller way, I knew what Neil Armstrong must've felt like when returning from the Apollo 11 lunar expedition, everyone asking him what was walking on the moon like, rendering himself eventually to his own self-imposed withdrawal from society.

I wasn't walking on no moon though, I was spaced out on thoughts of just walking into my own business premises. There was no let-up; wherever I went, the same questions would be asked. My life now was the shootings.

A short period of non-intrusion by the police soon came to an end one evening. One detective came to visit me in the gym, and he asked if he could have a word with me alone.

The quiet word was to see if I could attend the police station that night. If I wanted to bring a solicitor with me, I could. I had nothing to hide so I decided to attend by myself; what they did not tell me, my business partner was also asked to attend separately at the same police station.

There we were put under severe interrogation, in separate rooms, neither of us knowing of the other one's attendance.

Lines were set up by the police to relay my answers down to the other interrogation room to see if my answers corresponded with my business partner's and vice versa.

They also informed us we had both been getting followed, our houses monitored by cameras, our actions, what we did after being released from the police station were all relayed back to us. It was unnerving to think all our movements since had been under severe scrutiny, with not an idea by ourselves that our own version of *Big Brother* had been watching our every step.

Hours later, we were told we could leave; our answers satisfied the investigating officers of the law, if needed again, they would be in touch.

The now added weight of possible surveillance upon me added a new dimension to my crumbling mental state. Paranoia. The opening of my front door presented me challenges that stretched the fabric of my mind to breaking point.

Why couldn't I just lead a normal existence. A carefree walk down the road had been out of reach for more than half of my living years now. I had the ball chain of hyper vigilance imbedded into my DNA since the days of Arobieke, now its development into a full-blown paranoid state was complete.

The simple innocent phone call of a father saying good night to his children before they went to bed became a real possibility of an invasive one, not knowing if my phone lines were bugged. This was made almost certain when a detective went to use the gym's public payphone, with a sudden change of heart let slip our phone would have an interested third party listening.

Out the blue, with their own admittance, they were drawing a blank with all leads, then suddenly all potential witnesses were asked to attend an identity parade. The anxiousness of thinking I could be seeing the face of the killer again was once again another added pressure to join the long line of existing ones.

The first line-up drew a blank, but it still was a traumatic scenario to experience. My mind now was in need of help, I was in need of help just to function, so a visit to my GP was made, and a meeting with a councillor was set up independently. The doctor's answer was anti-anxiety medication; this rendered me into a zombie-like state. What was the point to throw a cloak over the problem, to not address the root cause? This was just as problematic as the issues I was taking the proposed medication for.

The counselling sessions got underway. To be fair to the lady who sat in silence during my slot of outpouring of sorrows, worries and tribulations, I think she became more and more traumatised by my story than me getting any relief from my openness.

Then came a breakthrough in the case, nearly four months after the shootings, once more we were asked to attend an identification parade.

As all the witnesses waited quietly in a room, one by one we were left alone to walk down the line of men appointed to stand in the parade, one of which would be the arrested individual, but would he be the gunman, only time would tell.

Kevin's common law wife Linda was first to leave the room, my business partner next, then I was the third to walk the line.

Once you had observed the line-up, a separate room awaited, there you would sit waiting, as the process of the other witnesses took their turn to visually overlook the occupants that stood between them and the one-way glass.

My back now facing the proposed row of subjects, I was given my instructions by the police officer in charge of the parade on how to view the awaiting line-up, to walk slowly, from the start, to the end and back again, even if the gun man was present, to still complete the viewing as instructed.

With this, I turned to face the line-up. I closely zoned into who was in front of me and proceeded scanning the line-up, walking slowly, giving every numbered individual my close attention, then with an abrupt halt to my observations, my eyesight locked onto one particular participant of the parade instantly.

I had seen this person in my mind for the past few months, every morning on waking, every evening going to bed, even in my nightmares, it was the gunman.

I obeyed the officer's instructions and walked up, then back down the line-up.

My heart racing with a fearful anticipation, at the same time a growing anger, a bubbling rage was heating up inside me, that the person that I was about to position myself in front of from behind the glass was the person who had fired the actual weapon that killed my friends.

The individual I was staring ice-like at, the cold fixed glare, was a carbon copy of the non-expressive frozen face that he himself portrayed on his slow deliberate approach before he carried out his dastardly deed.

The choice of his calculated monstrosity had changed the lives for many families; for many young children, it had left them fatherless. Turning my life upside down. Him pulling the trigger left two people dead. My injuries while not physical, were bleeding wounds to my mental state. My waited stare nullified any spontaneous vocal resentment from my mouth.

Asked now was the gun man there by the officiate, the defrosting immobilising muscles of my face and mouth positively, clearly and with sense of satisfaction replied, "Yes."

In a regimented clear command, he replied, "Give the number of that individual."

My duty to start the ball rolling for justice had been delivered.

I was then in the same sergeant major type of command asked to retreat to the appointed waiting room provided.

It turned out that the two witnesses before me, Linda and my business partner, had both picked out the same individual as well.

We left the venue of the identification parade in the same mini bus that had took us there, a somewhat jubilant atmosphere had joined us on the journey back to our drop-off point.

The knowing that another journey had just commenced, the road to a conviction of a cold-blooded killer, for the scales of justice from a jury hopefully to weigh heavy, tipping them in the direction of a rightful guilty verdict.

On our arrival back at our original starting-off point, I was called into one of the chief investigating detective's office.

Grey-haired, steely-faced contours trained to show no emotions, every bit of him fitting the part of a homicide detective you would conjure up in your imagination in relation to an on-screen DC.

Shutting the door behind us both, inviting me to sit down, the exhausted detective dropped, slumping down on his wheeled rotating chair behind his desk, a desk burdened with paperwork of other crimes, destined for his later underlying attention for a future shift of duty.

Elbows on his desk, palms of his hands supporting his forehead, the triangle shaped opening created a blinkered view of myself on the opposite side of the flat-topped piece of office furniture.

With a near breaking down of emotions, this hardened man of the law apologised profusely on the treatment that I had received from his department during the investigation.

If I ever heard or seen such a sincere, heartfelt apology, this was it. "I was just doing my job, Mark, I hope you understand that, we knew you had no involvement in the shootings, I am so sorry."

I held back tears for the detective's self-admission of wrongful treatment towards myself.

With his outstretched hand of an apology offered, I accepted.

This positive ID now left an imminent pending trial to take place. This would again pose other strains to my overall mental well-being.

What I thought was going to be a straight-forward trial, with a resulting guilty outcome, especially with the three crucial witness testimonies available to the prosecution, unfortunately would end up being nothing of the sorts.

Chapter Twelve
Trials and Tribulations

The trial, appointed to be held at Liverpool Crown Court, was to start around the November of 1999, over a year now from the shootings. With this, we became valued assets to Merseyside Police. On their worrying advice, with our status as pivotal witnesses in the trial, a suggestion of panic button alarms to be fitted in our homes and in the gym itself was put to us.

On pressing the little red button, the nearest armed response unit would attend the pin-pointed building or home, also in tow a sizeable squad of officers from Merseyside Police.

For the detectives, this was a precaution due to the fact that, in their own words, the monkey had been apprehended, not the organ grinder. Our sudden demise or non-attendance in court would possibly further protect their secrecy of involvement and any possible evasion of capture.

The post shooting reality was a grim one, being a witness in a gangland double hit posed severe worries and challenges.

The very real chance of attempts to hinder the road to justice by the crime lords behind the killings was one we had to give real consideration to, whether we were willing to put our lives at risk, not just pre-trial but post-trial, such involvement in a conviction would probably put a price on our heads or at least a bitter vendetta for life.

It was decided with the advice and unsettling encouragement from the detectives to have the panic buttons installed in our homes and business, another reality now thrust upon us in the ever-widening aftermath of the killings.

More disturbing advice would follow from the highly experienced custodians of the law, advice that would send the protective parental instincts of my wife and myself into overdrive.

Their sobering observations recommended that our two young children should be accompanied everywhere they go. This was obviously the case any way; my oldest child was seven years old at the time, so his journeys were chaperoned already by us, but now had to be made with even more heightened vigilance.

His school and teachers had to be made aware of the film script nightmare situation we were now facing. Our three-year-old daughter's pre-school years had just started; instructions to the school were that under no circumstances any one attempting to remove our children under the guise as a family member except my wife and myself should be allowed.

A stuck like glue to us attitude evolved, not letting both of our children once leave the gaze of our understandably sensitive overseeing.

My mind was still trying to find some respite after nine months of worthless counselling. I was still roaming the wilderness, lost in the up and down terrain of the treacherous landscape that was my thoughts.

My first attempt of sharing what was going on in my head was a resounding failure, but I was willing to try again with a psychiatrist. This would also turn into a resounding failed mission as well.

Sessions got underway with a not-so-enthusiastic doctor of the mind. The majority of the allotted time I sat in front of him, I babbled on about my woes, he meanwhile sat crossed-legged, slumped, twisting side to side in his pivoting perch, fumbled and spun his writing implement in his hand, scribbling shapes onto his notepad, counting down the clock of his precious time.

Eventually after a few non-productive sittings, it was concluded his services would have to be withdrawn. He was off to Iraq to warn the soldiers of the signs of P.T.S.D.

I was showing full-blown symptoms of the condition in front of him, and he thought his counselling and diagnosing skills warranted his expertise expansion to the Middle East, or maybe his mission was actually to perform for the troops with his unique act of twirling and catching his miniature baton in the form of a pencil, or displaying his abstract form of Picasso artwork to the delight of the British Armed Forces.

I begged to differ, his time with me though not worthy of his aforementioned skills no longer.

So without further ado, I carried on with the processing of my irrational way of thinking. Coping strategies would have to be developed by the architect of the now crumbling structure itself, me.

The detectives on the case wanted to prepare us for our appearance in Crown Court. I had already spent time in the witness box of a murder trial at the same Crown Court, that experience alone was horrific; the cross-examination from the defence barrister, the eyes of the whole court room and the attending press correspondence focused on your every word, your body language, your whole demeanour is under scrutiny.

Detectives warned me this trial would be subject to a huge media and public presence. The interest of a double gangland execution, it was a script made for a Hollywood film. For us, we were the leading roles for the pending media circus that would be lying in wait, ready to pounce, to pick up on any derogatory character assassination attempts by the defence.

This would absolutely be the case during the trial, over-dramatizing of the highest degree by Liverpool's own evening newspaper, big bold headlines that would put my own integrity to question by its readers.

To try and lead a normal existence, to be a father to my two young children and keep them away from the knowing of what their daddy was mixed up in unintentionally, was hard. A heart-breaking example of the effects it had even on my young family was now evident in their lives, not just the imposed restricted movements and constant chaperoning.

Sat on my settee gazing out onto my front lawn watching my children play innocently with the neighbour's grandchildren, who they had played regularly with all their young lives, in a nice place in my mind, overseeing the innocence of a childhood adventure of make-believe play out in front of me.

I remember smiling to myself thinking this what I live for. My children are my world. This simple pleasure was my real relief from the chaos of thought than ran amuck in my head.

Yet this was to be disturbed with an ushering away by hand from one of the grandparents of the children involved in the frolic of make-believe with my own children, then came the reprimand for the children getting led away unwillingly.

"What have we told you, you're not to play with Liam and Danielle again."

With an explanation needed, my wife confronted the grandparents of the children, why the friends' play time had come to an abrupt halt.

The explanation given, the reasoning behind the termination of the joy of playfulness.

They did not want their innocent grandchildren to be caught up in the crossfire of an assassination attempt on my life.

On hearing this, I headed upstairs to the bathroom, locked myself in, turned the taps on fully, with the noise of the gushing water, I tried to disguise my crying, my sobs of heartache, because of the explanatory comments.

Drying my face, looking in the mirror, I somehow quickly rationalised the grandparents' fear, that they were right in trying to protect their little cherished grandchildren.

It never made it any more easy to accept though. How my own children were getting punished for the murderous actions of a killer, the realisation of the now dire situation me and my family faced, this wasn't fair, totally unacceptable, the torment of suffering, the unjust cruel turn of events were not going to go away.

Was I going to make my life even harder by attending court to give evidence? Would it prolong this awful period of time by doing so? Were the innocent precautions of a grandmother in hindsight the reality of what could happen: an attempt on my life to stop me from bringing justice to the families of the two people killed in the shootings? I did have a choice to walk away and not attend the trial to give evidence.

The thought of the suffering the victims' families were enduring, the longing of the children to see their fathers again, the hurt and upheaval to my own life, this heinous act of the calculated taking of life, had to be made accountable by the actions of the gun man. I was to stand firm and attend to the daunting task and give evidence in the trial, that was now only just around the corner.

The unmarked police escort steadily made its way to Liverpool City Centre, passing the famed Liver Buildings in its journey before taking a left turn to go underground into the Crown Court, not the usual entrance for witnesses in a trial, only used generally for the judges and prisoners, but for us, the three main witnesses, this was the safest way to and from court. Our safe delivery every day by the police made the likelihood of the correct conviction for the crime essential.

Taken now up by lift, still escorted by the selected detectives that we were now familiar with, a special room was set aside for the prosecution's prized possessions.

All the trappings of a comfortable living room, television, comfy arm chairs, table, but noticeably no windows which made the four scantly furnished walls slightly imposing.

When the questioning request was asked could we be moved to a room with some natural light and fresh air from an open window, the unsettling answer was, unfortunately in such high profile and delicate cases just like the one we were in, that would not be possible, any windows would pose a possible threat for an assassination attempt, by either a rooftop sniper or, would you believe, a helicopter dropping down in front of the window, again with the intention of removing the witnesses with a bullet.

Shaking my head in astonishment and disbelief, surely the suggestions of such attempts should not apply to us. This was a crazy, *Die Hard*, Bruce Willis stroke *Godfather* scenario. On the same hand, analysing the possible threat, and the room we were now settling in, it now seemed very inviting and adequate seen in this different light.

The wait was agonising, made all the more nerve-racking as bulletins on the TV we were watching from the regional news programming gave up-to-date coverage of the trial from the comfort of our quarters.

A knock on the door from a court usher, signalled the judge and jury were ready to hear the first witness accounts of that fateful morning. It was Linda. She would be the first to relive the moments leading up to, during and after the slaying of her life partner and father to her four young children.

Hours passed, one day rolled into another, before the dreaded knock on the door of our base camp we had waited for came. Who would be next? The usher leaned in, "The court is ready for witness Mark Scott."

My heart skipped an anxious beat. The time had arrived to once again face a cold-blooded killer, to face the barrage of cross-examination questions from the defence, no doubt to see graphic photographs of the murder scene post shootings. I stood up with a big inhalation of breath, walking towards the door, my chaperone waiting to escort me to the awaiting court room.

Nerves now peaking, the sudden draining of energy, my mouth now void of saliva, at that moment it felt like I was walking to face the hangman's gallows.

I followed the usher into the lift. A feeble attempt at conversation received a one-word answer. I decided not to pursue any small talk, to just focus in my mind on the task ahead. Once on the desired floor, we headed to the appointed room of judgement.

The door was opened by the usher presenting a packed court room. Every available seat in the public gallery was taken, legal representatives from both sides, the jury itself, all had their undivided attention on me.

Trying to control my erratic breathing before I stood at the directed witness stand; deep steadying in and outtakes of breath remedied the situation. Once comfortably stood into the stand, I scanned the court room to get my bearings, to make myself aware of each and every faction present.

My eyesight was drawn to the screened-off part of the court room; behind it, sandwiched between to burly prison guards, was the rightfully accused assassin.

Speak loud and clearly were the instructions I was given by my inner self, the same instructions were then given to me again officially, as my hand was placed on the Book of the Lord.

The prosecution led the charge. The questioning was to build a picture up for the jury, the hour pre shooting, then the actual shootings. Placed on the witness stand, was an album; it was for my perusal. I was instructed by the barrister for the prosecution to open it.

A pausing abruptly stalled the momentum that I was building up in my answering the wigged official. On opening up the catalogue, the gruesome contents were revealed to me.

Lying there outstretched, the body of Kevin, a winded feeling embodied me. More to the point I stopped breathing due to holding my breath, the photographs in front of me were the identical ones that had appeared to me mentally, daily, ever since the incident.

I tried to claw into every part of my being so as not to fold, to buckle under the pressure, to show my fragile state of mind in front of the focused onlookers. My mouth now needed the lubrication of the water the glass in front of me held, sipping it, hoping the function of speech could resume.

As I gazed over to the jury unintentionally, I could see and feel a female member's pity for me as the documented pictures unveiled themselves as the pages were turned. My account of the events was delivered to the prosecution, truthfully and accurately.

The next day was the turn of the barrister for the defence to take centre stage. After my last appearance in front of such a legal representative, this was going to be an acute test to my character.

Braced now and ready for the barrister's first serve, a positive form of answering, direct and definite, flowed from myself. A harrowing realisation started to form within myself what the defence barrister was now applying to the members of the jury and the court itself, that it was me and the other two main witnesses who had planned the executions of the two deceased.

The absolute absurd form of defence I really wasn't expecting. The opposing barrister ripped into me about people known to myself, not as friends but certain people that I had dealings with regarding health supplementation that I sold in the gym, but were known in the criminal underworld. A very weak link, a grasping-of-straws attempt to undermine my clean untarnished character by the defence. I stood firm. The court was adjourned for the day, to resume the next.

The police chaperones returned me to the gym. With that I had a chance to see if the friends who volunteered to stand in for me in my absence were ok. Waiting on the off chance of my arrival outside the gym, an old friend was standing clutching that evening's edition of the city's newspaper.

Highly emotional, tearful in fact, he approached me. Walking and talking, he showed his out pouring of discontent, "How could they do this to you, Mark, how could they?"

With this, he showed me the bold headlines on the page:

GYM OWNER DENIES MURDER PLOT.

Astounded by the over-sensationalised form of journalism, feeling like another bully had joined the kicking of me when I was down, I despondently made the journey home. As I arrived to my front gate, an elderly neighbour's daughter was making her way into her parents' house. On seeing my arrival, she hurriedly tried to roll up and disguise her choice of tabloid. It was the same damning evening newspaper under her arm that I had just been shown outside my gym.

You already might've come to the conclusion what is so wrong with that. The fact of the matter was, the newspaper was not sold in my village, and that I now lived 25 miles away from the circulation of the tabloid. My immediate neighbours were keeping a close eye on my appearance in the witness stand, even going out their way to do so.

After my time giving evidence, I was relieved of my duty as a witness by the judge. Surviving this harrowing experience, I could now walk away never to return and hopefully a line could be drawn under the spotlight of being a witness.

It then became a waiting game, all the other witnesses had to be heard, the case for the prosecution, the case for the defence, all the objections, all the objections denied, before the jury could be sent out to deliberate, a foregone conclusion in my eyes. I had seen the accused with my very own eyes kill two men in cold blood, right in front of me. Nothing to deliberate – guilty!

In my front room, weeks after my last attendance in court, the jury had already been sent out to deliberate when the house telephone rang. The detective who was with me for the time I was in the assigned no-window waiting room of the court, said to me he would inform me straightaway as soon as the jury came back with a verdict.

Was this him, I thought, if it was, he would relay the inevitable news of a guilty verdict, any other decision had not really entered my thoughts.

It was the detective, but it wasn't what I expected him to say.

"Mark, I am sorry to tell you, the jury couldn't return a verdict, it has been declared a hung jury."

Not quite understanding the term hung jury, I questioned, "What does that mean?"

The reply made me slump down onto my armchair, as if the power supply to my body had been suddenly unplugged.

"You have to do it all again, in front of a different jury, a re-trial."

A few seconds' pause prompted the detective to ask if I was ok. This can't be happening to me, please no, I was thinking during the lapse period of conversation.

Completely drained now, mentally and physically, I questioned my own capabilities if I could go through the same ordeal once again. It was coming to the end of 1999, the new trial was now rescheduled for the May of the following year, another six months of uncertainty, but worst of all, if the last jury couldn't come to a verdict, would the next jury go one further and deliver a not guilty verdict.

This was totally unconceivable, but very possible, I had seen this person clear as day, feet away from me, shoot two people dead.

How could a jury possibly not believe that, not just my testimony, but two other witnesses. This just was not fair, this was the second time a jury had questioned my sworn oath, and not believed my account of the events that I was stood in the so-called witness box for.

An anger now replaced the disbelief and gave me the strength to fulfil my obligation and attend the re-trial, adamant justice would prevail.

The Christmas Eve of 1999 brought a brief relief to my constant thoughts of paranoia, and the emotions that were forever present whenever I was in the vicinity of my place of work, knowing that the next few days there would be an absence from returning to the constant reminder of the dreadful event due to the welcoming yuletide holidays.

This anticipated relief would be short-lived due to an unexpected visit, caused by the excited anticipation of the joy a Christmas Eve brings to young children.

My 8-year-old son would accompany me on this festive half day of work. The excitement of the day was brimming from my young eager work colleague, hopefully the day would also hold some playtime intermission with my business partner's son.

That was the case as they both snuck off up to the loft space of the gym. This overhead spacing was utilised like most loft spaces, for the hoarding of useless used bits of everything, but more importantly, it could be used by its two young inhabitants as a multitude of venues such as a football pitch, a school classroom, but in this instance, a circus tent.

A soft thick discarded mattress coupled with the height of a storage cupboard made the requirements for two over-enthusiastic young portraying acrobats to perform their somersault routines in front of their imaginary big top audience.

Little did the two innocent mischiefs know that the delicate receiver for our armed response reception committee was placed inside the cupboard they were using as launch pad for their double twist with pike manoeuvres.

The gym itself was full of members performing their last fitness stints before the inevitable over-indulgence the season of goodwill brought. In a Christmas scene straight out of *A Lampoon's Christmas Vacation* whereupon the armed SWAT team burst into the house to rescue the kidnapped boss of the accident-prone Clark Griswold, the armed response team burst into the gym to the horror of my exercising members, brandishing sub machine guns with a battalion of police officers behind them.

A very animated jobsworth constable took the centre stage to find the purpose of their deployment on what should have been an easy shift in his eyes. With the overtones of a disgruntled headmaster, he shouted aggressively towards me, "Who has pressed the panic button?"

Trying to think what the hell was going on, realisation dawned on myself that the two tiny tumblers upstairs must have accidentally triggered the device to unleash the firepower of Merseyside Police.

I quickly tried to submit an excuse for my son and his play mate. Not listening, the officer pushed myself out the way and headed up to the loft. On his arrival, he began to chastise the two children who were totally unaware of what their antics had set off.

Defence mode of a protective parent then embodied me, no one was allowed to speak to my son in the way he was without the right justification, police officer or no police officer. With that, I lost it verbally, dressing down the uniformed person who was now heading back down the stairs to the irate members of the gym.

As the specialised armed team began to realise it was a false alarm, they started to retreat. The last officer being the obnoxious bigmouth, out of sheer anger and frustration, a build-up of the tension the situation presented, I threw my set of keys, striking the officer on his back. This was greeted with a huge round of applause from all members, accompanied by a lot of verbal outpouring of discontent because of the treatment showed to me and the members of the gym by this one particular officer of the law.

Not a moment lost, I contacted the leading officers in the murder case and put in a formal complaint against the unpleasant uniformed policeman.

Action was swift, the officer in question was brought before his superiors, duties around the presence of the gym and ourselves were relieved from his work load and on any such reoccurrence of the alarm being raised again, he himself should not attend.

With this last situation unfolding, it brought an end to this troubled decade for me. Optimism for the new year was let's say shaky at best, but onward we went.

A déjà vu situation, coupled with the intense emotions of the last trial, but with an added nervous application of fear, was doused in my inner self. The complacency I had with the notion that a guilty verdict was the only outcome I thought could possibly be returned last time out, was now not the case. The repercussions of a not guilty verdict had not been addressed within myself, but did now have to be inconceivably considered.

My time in the witness box for murder trials, measured in hours, was well into double figures by the time my re-trial appearance had come and gone. The agonising wait for the trial to conclude, for the jury to be sent out, deliberate and give their verdict, was cruel to endure.

The fixed stare on the phone, in between the glance at the clock as the minutes ticked by, a verdict was imminent. The same officer as last time again promised to relay the news instantly as soon as the verdict had been delivered, to put me out of my misery or to start a newer type of one more unthinkable than what I was suffering at that present moment in time.

Breaking the silence of my front room, the startling noise of the telephone's ring sent the anxious butterflies of my stomach to flight. I presented the caller with a low volume, "Hello."

"Hi, Mark, it's..." The detective went on to do his polite introduction and then with no other build up, "It's a guilty."

The rush of relief, the tensing of my muscles that my fight or flight hormone adrenaline had produced, relaxed. The welling of the sodium-rich water broke the dam of eyelashes and saturated my cheeks. Justice had outweighed the scale of injustice, in turn sent the killer to a life sentence behind bars.

Or had it?

Murder in the first degree, a term used in the USA, meaning the crime exhibited some form of planning, premeditated, which was the case of the gym killings would've been categorised as, the punishment in most states carries a mandatory sentence of death or life without parole, this includes the States of California, Florida and a plethora of other states follow suit.

In other states, tariffs vary but become more severe if the offender's crime has multiple fatalities, has used a firearm in the crime, or has previous convictions with firearms, all these were applicable to the convicted killer in the murders I witnessed in my gym.

As I write about the effects of witnessing the event and the aftermath the trauma had on my life, changing it forever, twenty-three plus years have passed, not forgetting to mention the shattering effects it had on the families of the deceased, the convicted killer now unbelievably walks around as a free man.

After serving his term of twenty years as a convicted double murderer, that was premeditated with a firearm, this country's justice system released the killer back onto our streets, thinking that the crime committed justified the duration of incarceration and that it had been duly served.

In the blink of an eye, twenty years have passed; in that twenty-years, not one single day has ticked away without me revisiting the scene of the heinous crime in my head.

All thoughts generate emotions, the chain reaction is natural, that is the way the human body responds to the mind's nudge of thought. Your actions then respond to the emotions. If you on a daily basis think of the events I myself were subjected to, you reside in a very poor state of mental health. That's what you call a life sentence. Growing up without the person that you called daddy or soul mate, that's a life sentence.

So many times these variables are used by the victims' relations, friends and witnesses after lenient sentences are passed for such horrendous crimes, in this country especially.

Chapter Thirteen
Bullet-Proof Vest and Running Shoes

Post-trial saw the disappearance of the security of a police presence. This in turn brought added anxieties to the mix, the reassurance of a response team ready and waiting to come to your rescue was now gone when the police installation teams came and retrieved their panic buttons from my home and the gym.

An unease of uncertainty and paranoia plagued me on any stranger entering the gym with a sports holdall, never knowing if the contents were as sinister as the bag that sat at the feet of the gunman that fateful Autumn morning, but this was a gym and such innocent occurrences would happen on a daily basis.

Opening and closing of the business would become a flight or fight experience, leaving my vehicle or trying to return to it, thoughts of being shot or harmed in any other way would manifest in my head as I scrambled to open the front door of the gym. Even driving home at night was like running the gauntlet; on one occasion, I was driving down the motorway on my way home on an unlit part of the carriageway when a stone hit my windscreen. The bang and damage to the windscreen instantly conjured up a flashback with a state of realism an attempt on my life was underway. I dropped my head down between my knees and drove blind until hitting the hard shoulder, precariously missing a flyover pillar in the process. Still not sure if I was under engaging fire, I sped down the motorway shaking, gripping the steering wheel, making my knuckles go white till my forearms cramped up with the intense grip.

These were all post-trial realities, your honourable duty performed in a court of law now done, in a serious enough case for your own life to be put in jeopardy to attend as a witness, but now to be cast aside to deal with the aftermath of the whole harrowing nightmare by yourself.

No other person or persons were charged in the connection with the executions, meaning the people who had arranged the killings, who had brought the assistance of a hitman to the fold, were still at large.

Rumours post trial circulated, credible or not, that whoever had ordered the hit weren't happy with our appearances in court. Also an appeal would be launched by the killer, the removing of such witnesses for good would aid both courses.

These were whispers; in the real-life grand scheme of things, I had to take them seriously. The gathering momentum of such whispers came to head, which prompted action to be taken. Bullet-proof vests, extreme yes, but wasn't the life I had been catapulted into unintentionally extreme to say the least.

One such rumour that nudged us towards wearing PPE, was that an assassination attempt on mine and my business partner's lives was stopped at the very last hour.

The vicious rumour was that the gunman equipped with the tools of his trade, was travelling down from the North East of the country, apparently aborting his mission 20 miles away from the destination where me and my business partner were on this particular evening in question, totally unknown to us both at the time of this situation. It still could not be dismissed or taken with a pinch of salt eventually when we heard about the rumour.

This was the type of information getting fed to us periodically. Most of it was just dismissed generally due to the pigeon who carried the rumours being of the idiotic variety, but some snip bits of gossip like the one just explained, might've had grains of truth in. The delicate position we found ourselves in, we had to filter and decide whether it was credible or not.

The build-up of paranoia was etched into my DNA, after the relentless situations of acute awareness of my surroundings, due to circumstances out of my control.

My new form of fashion attire I wore in times of isolation away from other people or the times I thought I was most vulnerable, keeping the bulky protecting under-garment so not for people to suspect of my self-preservation aspirations was hard, as I sneaked in and out of it away from my children asking questions, was near impossible, after three months of looking like Herman Munster, I refrained from wearing the bullet shielding vest totally.

Still occupying a night slot on the front door of a bar and still housing symptoms of PTSD, on finishing work on a Friday and Saturday night, I would dip my toes or should I say dip my nose into the use of cocaine.

Again it brought an outpouring of contained thoughts to the people I gave an audience to, all sympathetic with the plight and weight I had to bear on my shoulders. This narcotic relief was becoming more and more of a self-prescribed therapy session, even the weekdays after work in the gym I would undertake a session.

I now had to take a close look at myself. During such a session and after, the paranoia would be frightening, the rumours of threats against my life would intensify in my head. I would relive the horrors of the deaths I had seen of people being murdered, now even greater, in more graphic detail, play out in thoughts I couldn't control.

It was time to take stock of a medication I knew that really worked, running, with a strict exercise and diet regime was always the only antidote for my glass-like mental state, with the added burden of stress due to my cocaine consumption, this pain of glass was about to shatter.

A plan of action now had to be put in place with myself.

The plan was to run the Rotterdam Marathon in 2000.

I would undertake the challenge of running 26.2 miles again with two objects in mind, a channelled focus was one, the other to generate charitable donations for another handpicked fundraiser.

This time it is was to bring a group of children over from the Ukraine, whose lives were still being affected by the Chernobyl Nuclear Power Plant Disaster some 16 years previous.

This organised effort was helped coordinated just like my past fundraising of the schools swimming pool, by my next-door neighbour, a true unsung champion and pillar of the community.

Once again, the build-up of excess weight had to be removed. Not having the same amount of time to prepare, I took the bull by the horns and got started supplementing my training with a road race most weekends.

This fell in line with my self-imposed guidelines of abstinence away from the lure of the crystal-like powder I was now indulging on far too many regular occasions.

This regime was working a treat, therapeutically rich in its reward, the Sunday worship in the form of a race meet was my form of religious prayer. I paid homage to the running saviour that was giving me redemption to battle the demons that had besieged my soul.

Notching up times now equivalent or just below my pre New York preparations but with the added handicap of around two stone, pleasing times, personal bests, all accumulated to a pleasing weather forecast of the mind, proven before and once again the vaccine against my unrelenting mental torture and its catalysis was always a pattern that prevailed.

At a body weight of around 15 stone 4 lbs, in a 20-mile race, I was crossing the finish line in 2 hours 43 minutes. In a torturous testing of my stamina a 30-kilometre distance up and down the North Wales hills in monsoon conditions was covered in a personal gratifying time of 2 hours 26 minutes.

My running companion and my own racing guru, who was my main source of reference in my fledgling years of the jog, a college lecturer, twenty years my senior, would become not just my running tutor but I suppose my parental guardian, warding me away from what the vices of our Dutch base camp had to offer, Amsterdam.

Rob my best friend and two other associates would also form part of the travelling contingent. They would accompany me and our appointed flag bearer, the very well-liked lecturer, Mr Whittle, hopefully cheering us on as we negotiated the marathon course in the Dutch seaport of Rotterdam.

For Rob and the other non-runners, this would be a chance for them to sample the delights Amsterdam had to offer, the likes of the Vincent Van Gogh Museum, the famous post-impressionist painter and the subsequent victim of fatal mental health issues himself, or the famed hiding place residence of Anne Frank.

Alas, all these world-renowned points of interests would all fall by the wayside, as the bright lights, or should I say the one bright light, the one being red, would take prevalence in their tourism itinerary. The cafes around the cities' canal systems and there delicacies of psychoactive pastries were also just too much of a lure to refuse for our enthusiastic entourage, for some in the entourage opting for a plant that was added to delicious batches of cookies was on the menu instead.

The marathon itself wasn't quite the success in time that I had hoped for due to an unprofessional sportsman's decision to purchase a tempting nibble off a street food selling vendor the night before the big race, which let's say paid me a revisit 15 miles into the marathon attempt, putting an end to the time goal I had in my head.

Damage limitation just to finish became the revised goal, not an impressive time on my stop watch, with the promised collections of donations in jeopardy with my near-on debilitating handicap soon became the most physically and mentally challenging race I had ever ran.

The remaining 11.2 miles were very precariously negotiated, but completed. My latest fundraising attempt again was a success; the children from the Ukraine had their holiday in the UK they were promised, some of which I met as my charity fundraising neighbours had offered their own homes as a place to stay for the young visitors from the infamous area of Ukraine affected by the radiation fall-out.

On both of my first two marathon fundraising missions, it was a real privilege to see the actual money that I helped raise used in my local community. The smiles and joy of the travelling children from the East seen first-hand as they undertook no doubt there first holidaying experience ever. The mental health boost to me was an added reinforcing bonus, the feeling of helping others, always presents an inner reward of well-being.

After this regime and mission concluded, no immediate focus was put in place, which in hindsight was a big mistake. What was planned though was a much welcome holiday for my young family, a dream trip to Disneyworld in Florida at the end of 2000.

Disney World's Imagineering was like stepping into the happiest place on the planet, not just for my children but for me. For two weeks I was just not on holiday, I resided in a world that I did wish upon a star to be in at my lowest times in my mind, back to the innocent times as a child.

This overwhelming feeling of happiness and joy was uncontainable one evening when we sailed towards the landscape of the Magic Kingdom on our appointed paddle boat steamer.

In the distance, the spires of Cinderella's castle stood out on the horizon. My young daughter was five years old at the time, in her Snow White costumed dress, she excitedly held the rail on the deck of the boat and jumped with joy.

Fireworks illuminated the sky, their loud explosions would usually catapult me back into a vivid flashback of a gun discharging its arsenal on route to end a life. For the first time since the shootings, my heart joined in the jumping with joy embracing my daughter's excitement.

A feeling I had not experienced for a long time, prompting tears to fall, this time not of torment but of thankfulness for the blessing that had been bestowed on me, that I was able to experience such a moment with my young family.

Walt Disney realised there was little grown-up in a child, but a lot of child in every grown-up. He had created an escapism from reality, not just for children, but for every adult. To this day, he has probably healed or soothed more people than all the psychiatrists in the world combined.

I have been fortunate enough to take my family over to the wonderful world of Disney on a number of occasions, at the same time escaping into the world of fantasy, leaving behind momentarily the struggles manifested in the real world.

Back returning to the real world, with it came the same symptoms of PTSD. Coupled with the wavering off course came the dropped guard, letting in the kidding quick fixes and distorted thinking of cocaine and alcohol.

My already fraying mental health was now getting help to completely tear the fabric of my mind. It was like throwing petrol on a fire, with the hopeless aim to douse the already established flames of vulnerabilities.

With me also withdrawing the strict exercise and diet regime, it was in effect like a type-2 diabetic refraining from a stabilising injection of insulin. If I was to look at my ups and downs regarding my mental health, the evidence strongly suggests, which will become apparent in the documentation in this book as a case study, the abstinence of a detailed form of physical exercise leaves my brain in a void of the mood-improving hormone, serotonin.

Chapter Fourteen
Rap Attack

My now consumption of cocaine was on the rise, visions of past events were becoming stronger, and my paranoia was off the rector scale on such binges.

The first half of the noughties was exactly that for me in regards to my behaviour. One particular delirious episode during this time stands out amongst some of the other most insane happenings.

The evening in question was spent alone downstairs of my old house, secretly snorting cocaine coupled with drinking large amounts of alcohol.

It became a game of two halves with me. I would put that much cocaine up my nose that my paranoid state would render me motionless, listening, watching for anything that to me was suspicious.

An example of being in such an acute stupor, in a trance of intent listening, would be when standing in complete silence, the noise of a plastic soft drink's bottle expanding after it had been held to pour drink out of, the seemingly loud pop as the crease in the plastic remoulded itself sounded to my distorted hearing like a gun had just been fired, making me jump out of my skin – ridiculous, I know.

To balance out this acute bout of hyper vigilance, I would consume more and more alcohol until I had levelled out and relaxed, then I would repeat the whole routine again: snort, paranoid, binge drink, repeat.

In the early hours of this morning, at the height of the acute paranoid state of the proceedings, I was stirring out my front window, peeping through tiny gaps in the window furnishings, on a curtain patrol surveillance mission, when a motor home of epic proportions pulled up randomly outside my home.

What happened next took my mind into believing me and my family were under an imminent threat of attack. Rumours were still circulating that an attempt would be made on my life, this made the situation all the more real to me and very viable.

Disembarking now from the impressive form of transport were a group of well-built adult males. On seeing this, I rubbed my eyes and shook my head, to somehow wake me up from what I was actually witnessing.

No, that didn't work. I shut my little peephole for a second or two then reopened it. The formidable posse were now heading for the small lane at the side of my house which led to a farm and the farmers' fields that were situated directly at the back of my property.

Who the hell, in the dead of night, could this possibly be? My deluded state quickly concluded they were here on a mission to kill me, the perfect secluded farmland to the rear of my house, a perfect point of entry for the forthcoming attack.

With this I armed myself. My paranoid state would not allow me to dial 999 due to the possession of cocaine on my person. I made my way into the kitchen with a commando type crawl, opening up the kitchen draw to retrieve a sharp enough implement which I could protect me and my family with.

Barricading the back door now with a dining room chair, I moved another one to the front door. Armed now with a bread knife and of all things a metal soup ladle, I positioned myself at a centralised point, where I could see and get to both entrances quickly if necessary.

I stood there as if I had been turned to stone, the only thing moving were my eyeballs side to side. My proposed plan hatching in my deluded thoughts was to run straight into the advancing enemy armed with my weapons of a bread knife and soup ladle before the ensemble of antagonists could advance any further into my family home.

Twitching, moving my hand back and forth to the latch of my front door to open it and just charge towards the advancing assassins, was a fraction of a second away from its instigation. With the flip of a coin in my head, I decided to protect and stay close to my wife and children just up the short flight of stairs away sleeping unaware of the happenings downstairs and around our property.

Also, my choice of weapons might not have been the most intimidating form of defence. My paranoia was now saying to me that my proposed assailants would just laugh at me brandishing my soup ladle and bread knife looking more like a psychotic chef than a well-equipped foe.

Standing now in the same position with a more suitable form of defence in my hands, a piece of wood resembling a bat, for what must've been hours, the now subsiding paranoia allowed me to look again through my peephole in the curtain.

To my bewilderment, the troop carrier of a motor home had vanished. Had I just imagined the whole last few hours? It was quite plausible considering the volumes of mind-bending commodities in my system, of alcohol and narcotics.

With this, I returned the kitchen wares to their rightful places and creeped up to bed. The next day I never mentioned anything to my wife about my near-on encounter with my imaginary posse of heavies and their hotel on wheels, until in the evening when my wife revealed to me some startling news.

My wife eager to reveal the headlines of the local evening newspaper called to me. "Mark, Mark, you'd never guess what…" were the words coming from behind the newspaper my wife was holding in front of her.

"Hang on a minute, I have something to tell you about what happened to me earlier this morning," I butted in. "It might've been something of nothing," I explained.

But considering the cloud we were living under regarding threats, the peculiars I had witnessed, that's if I never conjured it up in my out-of-tune pathological way of thinking, it needed to be said.

As I went through the events of the early hours, and how I nearly threw caution to the wind to go and attack the group of possible assailants, my wife shook her head at me, this same time calling me an idiot, as she exposed the headlines on the front page of the newspaper.

To my absolute shock, to my now questioning self if I was still in this crazy dream from the early morning mirage, the group of would-be attackers that I was going to throw caution to the wind and attack wielding my kitchen's top draw contents, was none other than the rapping/movie star 50 Cent and his posse G-Unit.

No, this chapter is not part of a figment of my imagination. I can understand your scepticism why the hell would you think this global mega superstar was wandering around a tiny rural village in Lancashire, in the North West of England, at the dead of night, let me explain.

On his journey up North, the M6 motorway being on his planned route, where one of its tributary junctions was near my village, after fulfilling a concert obligation in Manchester, G-Unit and their leader were heading to their next concert date.

Travelling in the early hours of the morning, still hyped up from his stage performance a few hours earlier, reciting his musical street poetry to the masses, often urges and inspirations for new material would fall from the sky to the rapping genius, with the impending urge in full flow, he apparently investigated by googling for the nearest musical recording studio.

Low and behold, unknown to me, one such emporium existed on the little lane to the side of my old house. With this, Mr Cent and his Units woke up the just as astonished proprietor and proceeded to record the lyrical inspirations that were running riot around his talented creative being.

Could you have imagined the headlines if I had undertaken my planned evasive attack. The mind boggles with the thoughts of what could've been if I would have charged G-Unit with the formidable armoury of a lethal soup ladle and accompanying bread cutter.

Chapter Fifteen
Car Bomb, the Loss of a Friend and the Spiral Down

My antics now, fuelled by an unsettled stability of the mind, nurtured with cocaine and liquid spirits like vodka, accelerated the decline in my demeanour. By 2006, I had been shown the door by my wife and told to go and stay back with my parents until I had sorted myself out.

There I would reside for a while until another harrowing destructive episode against my business happened, again with sinister intentions, it occurred in the April of that year.

Asleep in my old bedroom at my parents' house, I was awoken by a call on my mobile phone at 1.30am. It was a friend of mine who occupied the flat above the gym. Half asleep, I struggled with what my friend was relaying to me.

"Mark, you better get to the gym, somebody has blown the gym up, they have drove a car through the gym front."

"What?!" I replied in a just woken up tone to my speech.

The seriousness of the comeback was recognised instantly in my half slumber state. "Ok, I will be there as fast as I can," was the return to the panic-stricken voice on the end of the line. Jumping into my car still half dazed with the effects of sleep, I headed off towards the direction of the gym.

On my turning into the road, a glow of fiery orange midway down the buildings of family-run businesses brought me to the realism of the events that were about to unfold in front of me.

Fire fighters were engaged in a toe-to-toe battle with the inferno, as I arrived outside my cornered-off business premises.

The protruding back end of a car was just visible from amongst the raging flames as I looked at my life's work getting eaten up by this ferocious flamed dragon. On seeing the actual scene, I quickly found the person who was in charge and asked had everyone got out the building and surrounding properties safe.

"Everyone is accounted for, sir, and who are you?" the chief fire officer questioned.

"I'm the owner of the gym," I replied.

"Who have you upset?" was the worrying observation.

Policemen were now keeping bystanders away from the roaring inferno, one pushing me back as I tried to explain it was my business that was going up in smoke, then the vibration from my mobile phone grabbed my attention that was in my pocket – it was my wife.

My first thoughts were how did she know about the latest incident so quickly; after all, it was about 1.30am, not the usual time to make a phone call.

Presuming it was about the attack on the gym, I answered with the question, "How do you know about the gym?"

My wife's returning answer and request quickly responded me into summing the services of the policeman that was stood feet away from me.

In a distressed tone to her voice but at the same time trying to govern the volume of her speech quietly, told me she knew nothing about the gym. The reason for her call was that the CCTV cameras at home had picked up an intruder on our property. On my wife looking out of the upstairs bedroom window, she verified the camera's projections as the illuminating strips on the training shoes of the intruder on our property did him no favours trying to avoid detection.

Was this just a coincidence or was this intrusion tied in with the attack on the gym? All I knew was that my wife and children were under an immediate threat. The realisation from the police officer this was a credible cause for major concern, summoned the services of the Lancashire Police Dog handling division to attend my property virtually straight away.

Telling my wife to stay on the phone until help had arrived, to switch all the lights on, showing to the intruder he had been detected, it was an agonising time to wait for the police dogs. I was 22 miles away, helpless. Luckily, the cavalry were swift in coming.

On completing a sweep of the perimeters by the four-legged police operatives, they found no one. The trespasser had obviously thought twice about his intentions and disappeared. A huge relief, nevertheless.

My wife now put in the picture, with the uncertainty of whether this was just an opportunist house breaker or was it someone involved with the synchronised attack of the gym. Again, these notions were running riot in my now baffled head space.

In the morning as daylight gave light to the devastation, the true horror of what was intended could be seen. With it the sheer luck that had also prevented a scene of what could have been multiple casualties, possibly multiple fatalities.

Detectives yet again were gracing our premises, rummaging around the incinerated remains of the car used as the flaming missile, with a concerning look requested could he have a word in private with me and my business partner. These words off the investigating officer would send my consciousness into disbelief.

They led us to believe that this had nothing to do with the shootings, but then went on to reveal the full extent the arsonists went to, in an attempt to try and not just to destroy, but to kill any occupants of the building.

The stolen car that was used had barrels of petrol put on the back seats and in the boot. The petrol tank had also been filled to its capacity, the small family hatchback had been transformed into a weapon of quite considerable destruction.

The plot of the attackers somewhat failing only being foiled by the positioning of a steel beam at the front of the gym that halted the progress of the flying bomb. Heavy brick had replaced a foot on the accelerator pedal to give it the desired speed and momentum with a driver being absent from the controls.

The more chilling realisation was that literally inches away to the side of the charred wreckage was a gas main. If it had been ruptured to any extent, the row of businesses and there occupants above, would've been blown to oblivion.

Then came the descriptive advice from the detective, "Do you have any enemies, apart from the obvious that I can almost certainly rule out, being the shootings?"

"Are you involved in any feuds?"

"Have you upset anyone you know?" were the detective's line of enquiry, and then came his disturbing analysis:

"If you don't, the evidence certainly suggested it that the perpetrator's intensions was to cause as much destruction as possible, to the extent of killing anyone who was in this building."

He then went onto give some chilling self-observational recommendations.

"The best advice I can give you for the moment, is to sell your current vehicles. When you have changed them, drive around roundabouts twice to make sure that nobody is following you.

"Whoever is responsible for this well-planned, organised attack clearly means business," he concluded.

In a state of shock from hearing the detective's own perspective of our situation, this was something you would not want to hear even in the best of mental health, but I was already suffering with the acute effects of PTSD.

I was totally at a loss as to who would target my business with such murderous intent. Back now into the same predicament post shootings, but the damage a lot worse, the whole building never escaped the flames, even next door where we operated a tanning salon business had the devastating effects of smoke damage.

The clean-up operation had to be started straightaway. A new complete shop front of the building was needed, suspended ceiling, reception counter, upholstery of the weights machines and benches, and obviously total redecoration of the two buildings of business.

Once all the restoration was complete, again would members return like they did after the last atrocity or would this finally break the business? After all, the city's evening newspaper printed graphic photos of the gym up in flames with the headline 'Attack on Murder Gym' gracing its front page.

The lure of cocaine kept calling to me. All would be better if I sniffed the powder, the boost of confidence. The thoughts of structure on what I will do to remedy my problems, which all but lasted about 40 minutes after the drug had reached their peak levels of concentrate, then it was a steady fall into the pit of paranoia, extreme paranoia followed by the depressive state of comedown.

That was the merry-go-round call of cocaine I opted for yet again.

Anxiety levels, the lingering over-inquisitive paranoid thoughts ran riot in my already beleaguered state of play in my mind.

September of 2006 came around and yet another tragedy would push me to the point of rapid freefall. This type of premature tragedy would be hard to come to terms with in the best of mental health; for me, no rationalising, no reasoning, no justification in my unstable self would accept it – the death of my best friend Rob Bungie Blundell.

Our passion for boxing would be our last conversation, a bet in fact between us both; who would be the victor of that Saturday night's big fight. Sunday would always bring a quietening of correspondence between us both, due mainly to a recovery period from Saturday night's antics.

Monday came and drifted into the late afternoon with still no communication from Rob. After finishing my daytime Monday shift in the gym, I did a drive by of Rob's flat. Blinds still closed, thoughts crossed my mind that it must've been one hell of a Saturday night for the recovery period to stretch into Monday evening.

I arrived home, then shortly afterwards the phone call I will unfortunately never forget, the heart-breaking news that my close friend and confidante Rob had been found dead in his bed.

His friend and landlord who had the same concerns of non-communication entered Rob's flat to check on his well-being. His grim discovery was a shock to all the members of the gym and beyond, as news circulated fast about his passing.

I rushed down the motorway to his flat thinking I would receive the news he had woken up, that the diagnosis was wrong. A private ambulance and police car was parked up and a crowd of tearful friends had gathered outside of Rob's flat. In disbelief and in an eerie silence, Rob's body was wheeled out on a stretcher to the waiting dark ambulance in a body bag.

I carried Robin Bungie Blundell's coffin into the crematorium. With the eyes of over 500 mourners looking on, who had turned up to pay their respects on that September's afternoon in 2006.

He was 36 years of age. The void Rob left in my life was unmistakeably huge. A confidante, the lending ear and shoulder a good friend shares in your time of need, the strength I absorbed, which was doubled by our talks, was gone. The small things like the brief visits to the gym for a chat, the predictions of LFC's next game, what round would the victorious boxer's hand be lifted in the fight…

The knowing he would never walk through the entrance to the gym again, my phone would never ring and his name illuminate the handset, all these small happenings would be a huge loss in my life. The dark clouds rolled into my thoughts again with the added overload of storm assistance from narcotics and alcohol.

Breakdown would be complete in the March of 2007, when my wife would call for my GP to attend my bed side. His conclusion was for me to be taken by car straightaway to the nearest secure unit for mental health. There I would be assessed under the terms of the mental health act.

The journey was a blur. The day and time was unknown to me, even my own birthday was lost to my memory. My wife kept reiterating to me that I was going to be sectioned. I gathered some kind of equilibrium by looking at the dashboard of the car to register the time and date from the onboard clock. My birth date was repeated by my spouse as we pulled up to the unit.

A welcome committee of a burly nurse was what I was greeted with. Once in the building, the door was locked and secured behind me.

"Mark, I am not leaving you here, I can't leave you in here, you won't come out alive," my wife emotionally reassured me of her intentions.

"You must try your hardest to pass the assessment. If you stay here, you will get worse. I know you the best, I will nurse you back to health."

This pledge of devotion from my partner of the past twenty years nearly, showed the true traits of a remarkable person. Unconditional in her care, she had stood strong and tall in my hours of need, putting up with my emotional rollercoaster of mental health issues, my irrational behaviour and the other self-inflicted ailments.

Instead of just walking away, she sat next to me on that rollercoaster and fastened my seat belt to stop my inevitable unseating demise.

With these harsh words of reality ringing in my ears, the somewhat intimidating assessment got underway with the group of men in white coats.

The prediction of I wouldn't see the light of day again was a fair assumption from my wife, as the visions of what I had passed going into the scheduled meeting were the stereotypical goings-on in a mental health institution. Any period of time being forcibly held on one of its wards would've sunk this stricken vessel, not brought wind back into its sails.

As the burly nurse delivered me to my awaiting assessment of sanity, patients were lining up to be sedated with medication. A quick look to scour my surroundings of a ward through the circled windowed double doors, the sight of rows of beds with the empty cries of the people residing on them, brought the fitting sound to what my eyes had focused on, it was horrific.

I sat slumped on a chair in the corner of the doctor's office. A trio of mental health practitioners were present with my wife next to me. Simultaneously, the three doctors of the troubled mind reached to retrieve their pens from the lapel pocket of their white jackets.

A series of generic questions were put to me in my tested check-in, to probably what would've be a long extended stay in my medicating hotel Pilton, had it not been for the rehearsed answers on what I gambled what would be the questions prior to my admittance.

The difficulty factor of the questioning would not have troubled a six-year-old child. In my state of mind though the revision of the anticipated exam was the key to be let out of the secure unit I now found myself in.

A conflicting conversation of conclusion was openly discussed by the doctors in front of me. The slightly more agreeable decision of not for me to become an in-patient was decided. The look of relief on my wife's face was undeniable.

With the very same but surprised burly nurse from my entrance, he escorted me and my wife out, something that I don't think happened very often until a secure prolonged stay of treatment had been undertaken.

Driven back home, my antidote for such severe bouts would be to sleep in, which I undertook straightaway. This time was different on a waking up, I felt worse. My wife needed advice, so she phoned a helpline in which I was asked to speak to the person at the other end of the phone. The undertaking of talking to a professional stranger to discuss my troubles had always been a complete failure; unfortunately, this would be no different.

The person I am reasoning to believe had some sort of academic qualifications on the other end of the line in mental health issues; this however did not come across in our brief discussion together. With the counselling skills and the sympathy of a hangman, she discussed suicide and had I ever considered it. My reply was that such thoughts with any one suffering with depression were probably the norm.

Whether it was a gauge to see how bad my instability was, how far over that precarious cliff edge that I dangled over to carry out the life-ending act was, I don't know, but my answer was yes.

In a heartless reply coupled with a condescending tone to her voice, "Well then, why haven't you gone through with it?"

The chain of events resulting in this person's unprofessionalism added to the burden and very nearly prompted me to come close to the act of what the discussion was about.

Anger as if I was challenged by the lady to carry out the deed, I opened my garage, retrieved a saw, went into the garden, started to cut a piece of hose pipe of an adequate size to fit from the exhaust pipe to the driver's window of my wife's car, jumped in it and sped off towards a secluded wood nearby.

Off the beaten track now where cars don't go, I fitted the green pipe that would usually give life to a lawn or a flower bed with its contents, but in this case would channel poisonous fumes down it to encourage the ending of a life. Blocking the gap in the window with a towel, I reclined the driver's seat and closed my eyes.

As a light-headedness started to engulf me, I opened my eyes. A dog walker was approaching my car shouting, "Are you Mark?"

In a now fume-drunken state, I jumped out the car and dismantled the piping, not wanting this person to get involved in my pursuit of darkness.

I asked him, "Why?"

"The police are looking for you," he said.

With this, I headed off back home, turning into my road. On the corner there was a big blue tactical response van full of police, generally only seen outside football matches or major disturbances.

However, somebody saw fit to scramble it for use against a sad and bewildered vulnerable person.

Outside my house, I parked up on my drive. The awaiting officer approached me; I instructed him his services were not needed and closed the door behind him.

Now sat in my front room looking out the window, the big blue riot van rolled up, disembarking a host of burly police officers. I opened the front door to my house and stepped onto my driveway, giving them the same instructions that they were not needed and could they get off my property. Not even finishing my proposed speech, the leading officer pulled out an extendible baton and with full force, hit me over the head with it.

The force of the blow momentarily rendered me unconscious. Falling on the floor, I gained consciousness. With this, four male officers and one female proceeded to lay into me. My distraught wife, knowing my inner battles of the mind, leapt to my defence, throwing herself on top of me pleading with the so-called officers of the law to leave me alone, trying in vain to relay my fragile mental health issues to the licensed hooligans of the constabulary.

Pulled off me, she was met by a heavy restraint and a verbal warning from the woman officer that she would be arrested for preventing the course of justice if she didn't refrain from her protest.

Putting handcuffs on me like a tired-up hog, I was literally thrown into the small space at the back of the tactical response vehicle with the doors then slammed shut and locked.

The name Tactical Response Team, believe me the tactics of this squad of barbarians against a vulnerable person suffering mental health issues, who had just tried to take his own life, was just barbaric. The sheer dismissal of my wife as she tried to inform the uniformed aggressors about my vulnerabilities and my mental health condition, her cries of explanation blatantly and, now looking back, chillingly ignored.

During the journey to my unknown destination trying to fathom why and what had just actually happened, I questioned my treatment to the officers in the front of the vehicle on why it was necessary to strike me over the head with a baton. The reply, and I quote, "Because I was a big guy."

With this unacceptable response, I decided to play possum in the back of the appointed form of transport. The officer who bravely introduced me to his baton was sat in the front seat, trying to make conversation with me and getting no response.

I clearly heard them laughing in a self-gratifying way, the baton bearer himself discussing how hard he had hit me with great satisfaction.

On hearing this, I slumped to the floor, pretending there was something seriously wrong with myself. With this they pulled the big blue bus to the side of the road.

My plan, whether right or wrong, was to get some payback on the bully boy officer for the mistreatment he had inflicted on me.

I waited patiently for the bully to open the door to check on my condition. As soon as I saw a clear line of revenge, I launched myself towards him with the only form of payback weapon I had to my person, my teeth. On seeing the bare flesh of his cheek and ear, I launched myself at him.

With the likeness and propulsion of a great white shark targeting a seal off the coast of South Africa, I exploded out the back of the van. The self-proclaimed air jaws attack was a failure, as I landed flat on my face in the road.

Bundling me back into my crate, we carried on with the journey to the waiting committee of more officers at the police station, who all joined in their fun of choking me and driving knees and elbows into my body then throwing me into a cell.

With no formal explanation of their tactics and why they were called in the first place, hours later they let me go. Confused, I walked a short distance before my wife picked me up. Suffering with an excruciating headache later that night, I decided to attend the local A&E.

Still irate about the treatment I had received earlier that day, to my own admission totally out of order and character, I aimed my frustrations towards an officer of the law outside the hospital. Threatened and scared by my behaviour, he rightly emptied a whole canister of CS gas on me, rendering me in a heap on the floor. Carried now into another waiting police van, I was taken back to the police station I had only just been released from hours before.

This time the welcome committee punched and beat me all the way into the same cell I had resided in that afternoon. My eye closed over and swelled black and blue with the blows that rained down on me.

I totally regretted my actions towards the officer at the hospital and deserved to be punished by the courts, but my treatment by the other law enforcement officer was totally unjustified. Later cases of brutality from officers of this station would make headline news, with convictions and themselves spending time behind bars.

In 2015, I would be invited by the probationary services to attend a conference on the treatment of mental health sufferers who had been arrested during acute periods of their sufferings, their treatment and care, or should I say lack of care and compassion by the police. These would be the topics of conversation to be addressed at the London's Canary Wharf venue. Some of the tales from the participants attending the meeting were genuinely horrific.

More and more cases of barbaric treatment towards mental health sufferers by the police are starting to emerge, one recently was of an ex professional footballer, Dalian Atkinson, dying because of the beating he received from officers during his arrest in 2016 while suffering mental health issues.

Tasered over six times and kicked in the head at least twice, the officer who inflicted the fatal beating was sentenced to 8 years for manslaughter. In my eyes a verdict of murder should have been delivered. His accomplices, other officers including a woman P.C who used a baton on Mr Atkinson, is at this point in time still having her first trial, the jury being discharged having not been able to deliver a verdict.

Myself, the court heard how out of character it was for me to act in this way, with 38 years of a clean record and my mental state regarding the events that had been bestowed on me, I was fined and given a two-year probation period, which I totally accepted; this also came with a house arrest order of four months which I duly served.

The court also advised I should seek help with my mental health issues, substance and alcohol abuse. The only remedy that worked all the other times, running and raising money for worthy charities. With this antidote of the self-prescribing regime, I set my sights on a return to New York in 2007 to run the five boroughs again.

This plan of action also brought me together with a new best friend and running partner, who joined our family unit in the April of 2007, my little Boston Terrier dog, his name given by us: Bungie.

A tribute to my passed best mate, leaving no legacy when he died, no children, I wanted to keep his name alive, to say his name every day. In doing so, we kept thoughts of my great friend fresh in our memories, 14 years on, this is still the case with my life-changing four-legged best friend Bungie, the little Boston Terrier.

Chapter Sixteen
Reliable Remedies

With my running shoes dusted down, I hit my favourite trails, exploring the woods and flora with my new training partner Bungie. With the stamina of his long-distant cousin, the wolf, still exhibiting in his tenacious character, he would easily cover the long training distances, while I was exhausted on finishing such a run, my little four-legged friend would be willing to do it all over again.

Three huge antidotes were now in place to do battle with my enemies of PTSD, alcohol and drugs; they were running, embracing the natural environment on my runs, and my new constant companion Bungie the Boston. This treble whammy against my foes was like a round-the-clock cloak of protection.

Myself and my youngest brother James would tackle the Big Apple course, but this time my wife and two children would make the journey across the pond to cheer us on, the chosen charity the MS Society, selected due to my brother James's now ex-wife being diagnosed with the dreadful condition a couple of years previously.

A few months prior to us leaving for New York, I was given a quite remarkable and generous invitation by one of the world's biggest drug traffickers of the 1970s and '80s, George Jung.

George was the main character portrayed by Johnny Depp in the blockbusting film *Blow*. The film tells of his involvement with the Colombian Medellín cartel, headed by the infamous Pablo Escobar. It's the story of George's amassed wealth through the exportation of cocaine from Columbia into North America, coupled with his just as dramatic fall and the destruction of lives including his own that the category A drug inevitably does to all its acquaintances eventually.

After first watching the film, the core of its meaning resonated with me and prompted me to speak to George personally. At the time my life had been turned on its head all down to the one denominating factor, cocaine, used as a self-prescribed antidote for my P.T.S.D. Its marks were also on the gangland murders, the premature deaths of friends, all of which had the stamp of the South American cartel's export all over them.

George at the time resided in FMC Devens Federal Prison in Ayer, Massachusetts, USA. In one letter George wrote to me, in his own way, he analysed his life and mine in quite an observant unusual stand point. It went like this:

Sir Mark,

You're an unexpectedly poignant man.

Both of us have lived Ribald fairy tale meets Apocalypse Now lives and lived to tell the tale about it.

We have dared to pull the false moustache of the world and reveal the even greater mystery underneath.

Life is truly an ocean and every ride a phantasmagorical wave.

I believe in forever knowing it will never end.

The secret of the sleeping rose is that it believes in Spring.

Pruned, it will bloom again.

I love your damn country and its people – "Never say never!"

Experience and knowledge befit wisdom.

I look forward to your November marathon.

I offer you to speak with my friend, Sir Bo Phillips, living in Cape Cod, so that we can give you a grand welcome.

Telephone: ------------

Ask for Heidi or Bo.

P.S.

Also feel free to speak to my lady love, Isabella.

Tel: ------------

You must visit Miami and South Beach.

Great hotspot."

I always got a sense of regret but hope for the future as well from George's words. A quote he used in one of his pictures he sent me from Devens, read:

"Life is like a fine wine,

To sip and remember."

George was certainly a very poignant man. Unfortunately, I never took up George's kind invites, I wish I did. Just before the offer, I booked to stay with my family in an apartment in Manhattan while we were in New York, booked hastily over the internet, afraid we would have nowhere to stay because of the amount of people looking for accommodation over the Marathon weekend. I paid in full on a credible website. Unknowing to the hosts of the website, the apartment did not exist; I lost the whole amount paid of £2500, the scammers knew exactly how to play the people coming from overseas, most running for charities, the scammers truly despicable, vile people.

So, travelling to Boston became financially unviable. It was such a pity. George was released from prison in June 2014 after nearly 20 years. He sadly passed away at home in Weymouth, Massachusetts in May 2021. I never did get to meet Boston George personally but his kind words and invitation I will always remember, giving me inspiration and encouragement through a very difficult and troubling time.

I had been back to New York before my latest attempt at the marathon course, in 2004 for a Christmas shopping trip with my wife and children and my business partner's family. Whenever I am in New York, it always leaves me with a tale or two to tell. Just like my soup kitchen episode back in 1997, the next visits also held tales, one was a Central Park ice skating tale in 2004, the other a yellow New York cab journey that was truly unforgettable.

The skating tale was at the famed Christmas Trump sponsored ice rink in Central Park. Unfortunately, I am not blessed with the natural skills to balance on two steel blades and glide around on rock hard ice in an orderly manner, far from it.

The willing participants from our two families, which were only my children, my business partner's children and his wife, donned the boots with the idea to gracefully in one direction follow the other skaters around the rink and soak up the spirit of Christmas the city's famed attraction and woodland were oozing.

The only thing I would be soaking up would be the puddles of melted ice through my backside, as my attempts to stay on two feet were more likened to a drunken baby giraffe that had had its fill of the favoured Christmas alcoholic beverage of eggnog.

Now being held up by my daughter and my business partner's wife and her daughter, this was still not enough scaffolding to stop my dire attempt to skate two steps forward and not to bring the three of them down with me. For the life of me, I could not string a sturdy two-step glide together no matter how hard I tried.

My prancing on ice had not gone unnoticed by the law enforcers of the rink, the dreaded ice rangers of Central Park.

As I picked myself up for the umpteenth time, the eyes of an ice ranger were firmly fixed upon me. I am also now going around in the wrong direction causing mayhem with the more competent skaters. I was a now a human bowling ball for the other rink users who were the skittles.

The ice ranger picked up his pace towards my direction, on his arrival the direction of his comments were not made towards me but my business partner's wife who was hauling me up, trying at the same time to steady herself, not just trying to save me but to save her now own dwindling dignity along with her daughters and my daughters.

Shouting now, the disgruntled guardian of the ice relayed his message of discontent, with the directional telling off to my chaperones of the ice. He instructed, "Excuse me, ma'am, adults with special needs," meaning myself, "are prohibited to use the ice."

On hearing the ice ranger's observational remarks, I ensured him I had no special needs, not even able to finish the sentence. I could feel my skates giving away again. With this, I grabbed the official by the lapel of his uniformed ice ranger jacket to stop my inevitable fall.

In the attempt to keep myself upright, he joined me on the cold, wet slippery ice of the rink, a place this expert skater had probably not seen in a horizontal position since his novice days of learning the techniques on how to manoeuvre gracefully on frozen water.

My inability to grasp any type of simple sequenced steps prompted a host of rink officiates to carry me off the ice, to the howling laughter and non-sympathy from my wife and business partner, who watched on with extreme amusement from the side-lines.

Getting back to my 2007 NYC marathon attempt, another episode quite nearly could've put paid to our fundraising before it had even started.

After attending the Marathon expo, where me and my brother had picked our number bibs and timing chips, myself, my brother, wife and daughter would hail the iconic NYC yellow cab from outside the expo.

Hand aloft waving to a host of the yellow passenger carriers, one suddenly caught our attention and made his way to the side walk to pick us up.

An Italian gentleman, who would not have looked out of place on the set of *The Sopranos*, would be our pilot back to our hotel on 42nd street, The Grand Hyatt, which had been one of Donald Trump's first projects in Manhattan, his estranged wife Ivana then turning the ram-shackled property into the now flourishing hotel it is now known as today.

After our requested destination was submitted to our ride, he put his foot down literally to the floor and sped off into the flowing every-man-for-himself traffic of the city, myself in the front passenger seat. I quietly turned to my family in the back and gave the instructions to buckle up.

We zig-zagged in and out of lines of traffic with inches to spare, when suddenly a truck played the rude game of cutting in front of us, the same game our driver had been playing since the journey began.

This did not go down to well with our chauffeur, in his fiery Italian temper, he began to hail a barrage of obscenities to the truck driver. I must admit, 'you motherfucker' has certain elegance and conviction to it when spoken in Italian.

The truck now, not the driver, got the brunt of the frothing Italian driver's anger, which he proceeded to ram into from behind repeatedly. The action unfortunately was a mismatch for the little yellow cab; it was like the driver was banging his head against a brick wall, he was the only one who was going to come away second best, in this case it was the car's front grill.

Braced with my arms now outstretched on the dashboard to buffer any more collisions, I looked into the rear of the cab to check on my family, who had like myself took up the brace position in the back, all with a wide-eyed look of astonishment on their faces.

Our irate chauffeur was now trying to lean out of my window to grab the attention of the truck driver as he slipped alongside of the formidable haulage vehicle, giving it a side swipe in the process while I was trying to lean over to the driver's side as not to become part of the intended squashing.

With one last side swipe at the truck, our destination required us to turn down a separate street, with an obligatory middle finger salute, the driver calmly repositioned himself at the helm and resumed his captaincy of the vehicle, thankfully our hotel was only now a block away.

Pulling up over on the other side of the street from The Hyatt, as soon as the cab came to a standstill, my family, the occupants from the rear, disembarked with a haste as if Tiffany's that was situated just around the corner were giving away free diamonds.

I was left in the front to sort the fare out for the impromptu white-knuckle ride, which might I add, in my typical English attitude of not to complain, gave the driver a sizable tip for his trouble and thanked him.

With that, off he drove into the shoal of yellow cabs, disappearing under the cover of the concrete sea of sky scrapers.

A damage assessment then took place between me and my family on the side walk, to see if there had been any injuries from the turbulent taxi journey, whiplash to the two runners could have possibly side-lined our participation in the race before the starter's gun had even been fired.

Luckily, a sprained thumb was the only injury picked up by my brother between the four innocent occupants of the cab, due to us riding with the deranged New York Italian stock car driver.

The marathon was a huge success for us all. My brother and myself raised a considerably large sum of money, over £6000, for the MS Society, my intention to get around the course at my weight of 17stone 3lbs completed in over 4 hours 35 minutes.

The sight of my wife and daughter cheering me on at the finishing line in Central Park is a memory instilled in my heart forever. Just like the traumatising events I have witnessed in my life, I also have the ability to remember the times when the rewards of life paid with this sort of priceless moment.

Running the final few 100 metres in the famed park, out of all the thousands of shouts of encouragement, I picked up the voices of my wife and daughter.

Turning to my left, like an in-built visionary guidance system, I locked onto my cheerleading family amongst the other enthusiastic supporters, running over to the crowd control barrier, my vision now obscured by tears, my speech impeded by the lump of emotion I had just swallowed, I embraced them. After the brief relief from the constant hours of motion, my wife gave the instruction, "Go on, finish!"

Not just being there encouraging every step in the 26.2 mile race, they had been there more importantly behind me picking me up then propping me up, steadying my footsteps through thick and thin during my turbulent journey to stability.

Chapter Seventeen
A Cry for Help, and Policia
and the Bandito

The following years I would try to keep some sort of regimented exercise routine. This was helped very much so by the additions of a female Boston Terrier puppy we called Phoebe and the subsequent puppies she and Bungie produced; out of the six pups, we kept two.

Lucky to live in a very rural area, walking our family of Bostons in the woodlands and trails was like having a daily dose of sheer pleasure. The excitement and playful happiness of our pack would be infectious, with the added pleasure of walking and talking to family members on the same hikes through the countryside that no doubt would not have occurred without the accompaniment of our four-legged family members.

The love and loyalty this tiny breed of dog showed was truly therapeutic. After reading about the breed's history after my pack had already been assembled, this first all-American breed of dog was used for the purpose of convalescence for, would you believe, sufferers from PTSD.

With no doubt in my mind, they helped me sustain long periods of good mental health and abstinence from addictive short-term euphoria producers of the liquid and of the powder variety.

One obstacle I couldn't seem to overcome no matter how hard I tried, were the feelings of separation from my comfort zone. On leaving my house, to go back near enough every day, was to the scene of the shootings, my workplace, the gym, years later still held horrors in my mind that would resurface every time I would enter the building.

Every time I would mop the rubber gym mats where one of the victims died, visions of the clots of blood I had to clean up never faded. If anything, they became more vivid. Cleaning the changing room where the other victim fell, the same scenario would enter my train of thought, scraping and mopping up dried pools of blood.

Putting on a brave face, keeping a lid on my true feeling of discontent, was now becoming over-bearing. Rob gone, no one ever replaced the confidant that was him.

Another long-term friend, the friend who took me to one of my early bodybuilding contests in Crewe Cheshire back in '86, was again training at the gym that little bit more now. It was nice to see Eddie on the occasions he popped in for a chat.

On this early morning, I was half asleep in bed when my phone bleeped indicating there was a text message waiting to be read; quickly glancing at the text, it was from Eddie.

Could I please contact him if I didn't mind, it read, he needed to speak to me. With it being the early hours, I thought he might have had a few drinks, so not being on the same wavelength, I choose to ignore the message.

Twenty or so minutes later, the bleep of the phone's warning of a message sounds again, this time another request to call him but with the added request of not to tell anyone about him speaking to me; still in a state of half sleep, I thought about the request but drifted off into a deep sleep.

Getting ready to go to work that afternoon, my phone rang. I half expected it to be Eddie telling me what he wanted to speak about; it wasn't Eddie, it was a mutual friend of mine and his. He rang me to deliver the news that Eddie had took his own life, he had hung himself.

The feeling of guilt, of not answering his cries for help embodied me. I sat on my bed in disbelief. 'What if' was at the starting of every thought in my head. I had failed a good friend in need. Of all the selfish acts, forgiving myself was hard to come to terms with.

Friends told me that I wasn't to know what his intentions were. It still brought little solace to me, after all that I had experienced, and was still going through, I should have recognised the signs of inner hurting.

Now another tragedy I would associate with the gym would play on my mind, the tempting lure to injure just going the gym now would rear its destructive face again – cocaine.

The weakness of my thought exposed my demon, jumping all over for the notion of a rewarding measure of the fast fix of dopamine, and so the habit resurfaced, with the reasoning behind it to just face up to going into the building that held torturing flashbacks of past events, people and heart-aching memories.

Breaks from the gym would be most welcoming in the shape of holidays with my family and even some with my son and his friends who were all now in their late teens early twenties. The trips to a friend's villa in Portugal would become ones to remember the most. Again, these short breaks would not go without a tale or two. Here's one that still brings tears to the eyes to the people I relive it to, so let me tell you the arresting story.

This particular day started like most others in the roomy villa situated in a plush golf resort near Vila Moura. The drinking table on the patio would be set up accordingly, on it would reside the usual hardcore spirits of Grey Goose, Jack Daniel's and Jägermeister, all in quantity, with the odd box or four of the preferred chilled beers.

The preferred card game that would occupy us through the day, would be a rebooted version devised by ourselves, of the TV show *Play Your Cards Right*. The Cards in this instance would be ones of the explicit nature. We renamed the game 'Bush Cards', due to the 1980s and 1990s models' lack of attention to their pubic region, hair that would not have looked out of place on top of Donald Trump's head or a young Michael Jackson's.

After an afternoon session battling with the Bush Cards, reciting the words higher and lower, some of the participants were lowering their heads down the toilet as the pace of drinking started taking casualties.

Early evening presented itself with three survivors left from the day's frolics of Bush Cards, me and two of my son's close friends. The three of us then decided to head off to the marina area to where we would seek a change from our card game that had amused us all day.

Our quest for a different form of amusement was quickly found with the choices of bars and the likes a plentiful on the marina. After a short discussion of what route of amusement we should take, we unanimously decided it should be the local gentleman's club, the alias name for a lap dancing bar, a particular establishment my young companions had never frequented before.

There first experience of a seated dancing experience would turn out to be an arresting one, so here is the tale of:

POLICIA AND THE BANDITO.

On arrival, the two shy and naive young men sat sheepishly down as myself chatted to one of the employees of the establishment.

A Brazilian national with a likening to that of Beyoncé Knowles, with a derrière to match. We got on like a house on fire, making her laugh with the tales of my past antics. With her being relaxed and at ease with my persona, she invited me for a free dance down the stairs to the club's private booths. Slightly hesitant to her invite, after all, I was only trying to entertain my son's two young friends.

With the encouragement now of my two young wingmen, I accepted and followed behind the exotic dancer, where on I noticed the extremely round and pert bottom even more than before.

On sitting me down in the velour seated booth, the dancer closed the curtains, a piece of music started playing and with this, shapes of her profession in the form of dance followed.

Then came the weird request: could I sandwich my hands together for her, as if I was about to say a prayer. I sat slightly confused.

With my hands now in the prayer position, fingers pointing towards the dancer, she turned swiftly so her back was facing me, more to the point her bottom was in direct alignment with my outstretched hands of prayer.

In a more suggestive tone, with a hint of authority, she said, "You bandito, me policia."

She then parted her pert cheeks of her bottom open and reversed onto my hands, snapping shut her cheeks of steel, rendering my hands locked tight in a butt cuff.

With this and the repeating of the "You bandito, me policia" statement in a now more aggressive tone, I started to exhibit my built-in traits of paranoia as she led me around the room attached to her butt.

Who was this, I thought, was it an undercover Interpol agent, why did they want me? Totally embarrassed and afraid, she opened the curtains and proceeded to walk me up the corridor that was the main walkway for the row of curtained-off booths.

I tried in vain to release my imprisoned hands from her arsenal of restraint, pardon the pun, but for the life of me, I could not pull my hands free to release myself from her clamped shut tight gluteus maximus.

After a lap of the corridor, with bouts of twerking in the process, the relaxing of her derrière unlocked the shackles that had left me to her beck and call. She burst out into fits of laughter, I collapsed to the floor in a heap.

The joke was on me, the arresting technique of my apprehender was in fact her renowned party trick she began to reveal.

As we headed back up the stairs, then a wicked notion passed through my devious mind, so I shared it with my arresting officer.

I filled her in that my two young associates could do with a baptism ritual on it being their first visit to such a venue.

Only too willing, she led my sons, two highly excited friends, one at a time, down to her arresting dungeon lure, where the excitement of the young detainees quickly evaporated into sheer horror as she proceeded to read them their rights arresting them accordingly, subjecting them to the butt cuff, detaining routine of the Brazilian Policia.

Chapter Eighteen
The Road to Psychosis

With my remedy and reward for just being able to face the effects of PTSD, to just go and do a simple shift in my place of work, cocaine was the carrot I dangled in front of my nose, to reward myself after each shift. This obviously became an overwhelming problem, bigger than ever before.

I had tapped into my primal instincts, my reward system to seek out the drug, in the same way a primitive human being would have had the desire to seek out food and water in a hostile and dangerous environment. It was well worth the risks with the powerful rewarding hormone dopamine awaiting.

The way I was tuned in now, my dopamine pathways were actually now secreting before taking the drug. The thrill of the hunt or the chase if you like, my pattern of thinking once I had decided to seek the company of cocaine, there would be no turning back. It was only on very rare occasions that I would refrain from my quest. The way this powerful plant based derived chemical had messed up my indigenous pathways for pleasure was devastating.

I had more euphoria prior to taking the drug than I had when I had actually snorted a line of cocaine. Even when I started to devour my prized purchase, the intense peak was short-lived, 20, 25 minutes at the very most, then the quest would be to chase that elusive feeling again.

Subjecting myself in the battle to the extreme waves of paranoia would be the next stage in the sequence. That's where alcohol became more and more into the equation, as the paranoia replaced the euphoria.

The paranoia was subsequently doused by the effects of intoxication due to the amount of alcohol I would try and drown the effects of the frighteningly acute awareness, and so the vicious circle would start all over again.

An example of a bout of extreme paranoia was when I would lock myself into my office of a night time. When a wave of paranoia would engulf me, I would literally stand in one spot for up to four hours at a time looking through the blinds into my back garden.

On one such occasion, I had convinced myself there was someone standing in my garden with an axe looking up at me, my rational train of thought had abandoned me.

What I was actually looking down at for 4 hours was a replica suit of armour that held a medieval battle armament in its hand that was positioned in my garden as ornate garden furnishing. Every time I would enter the acute state of my paranoia, I would convince myself there was an intruder on my property.

Even before I started snorting the acquired batch of cocaine, I would tell myself there will be no one in the garden. It's Arthur, I would reassure myself standing there holding the medieval axe – Arthur was the appointed name for the suit of armour that stood to attention in my garden and the route to my intense glare of concentration spanning hours.

My paranoia would always override and kid me into the world of imaginary happenings. When I would finally actually go to bed, I would then stare at the large screened television that the CCTV cameras I had monitoring every corner of my property were relaying back from around the boundaries of my home.

With bulging eyeballs resembling two poached eggs, at times my vision was so sensitive that when the *Big Brother* night vision cameras would pick up the reflective eyes of a small field mouse, my paranoid behaviour would make me believe it was some type of roaming device spying on me from the shrubbery of the flower beds. Psychosis was slowly embodying me, with traits of the condition now showing in between my office binges.

Quantities of cocaine that I would take in one go were ludicrous; in my various stages through the years of taking cocaine, it was not unusual for me to divide into two lines, one eighth of an ounce of the powder, and snort each line into my nostrils one after each other.

Putting that amount in layman's terms, the usual sale of cocaine to the average recreational user would be a quantity weighing 0.5 of a gram, that purchase would probably see the user adequately supplied for the evening; my consumption was seven times that amount, just in one intake.

The result of such actions would dangle me over the cliff edge of over dose; in fact, looking back now, it's truly a wonder my heart didn't malfunction in some sort of way.

That couldn't be said about my mind, that would certainly malfunction, it would be like a joining of two super powers, drug-related psychosis would manifest itself with my already battle-worn PTSD condition, I had created the perfect storm.

The effects of my condition resulted in actions that would have been certifiable in the eyes of any mental health operative. An example of one such episode was the eating of a chip; now you might say that's not mad, the consuming of the tea time staple delicacy, but it is totally bonkers when it's a phone chip, the sim card out of a phone to be precise.

This outrageous behaviour in my head was the best way to get rid of any incriminating evidence of my dealings regarding the purchase of my cocaine from the sources stored in my phone.

My already anxious demeanour, being around people was getting worse. Even with a modicum of cocaine still in my blood stream, my anxiety would be deemed acute. Gossip on the streets, idle or not, about repercussions all these years later from the murders in the gym, would add fuel to the fire to my nervous disposition.

So at the end of 2013, just before going into the new year, I would again try and banish my demons, so once more I fell back to my reliable form of medication, running and a more constructive dieting regime.

With my four little Boston terriers in the isolated woodlands, was where I would lose myself in the peace and tranquillity that the countryside, my own little Eden, had to offer.

At over 19 stone, I was at my most unhealthiest I had ever been in my life, physically that is, mentally I wasn't far behind in the stakes of being at rock bottom. Going into the Easter of 2014, weight was dropping off me; in fact, I had shed around 4 stones. The reliable antidote I always fell back upon was again working, but with the added absence of the daily dose of high calorific alcoholic drinks, this aided with the quick weight loss.

All this hard work would come crashing down around me when a thank you gesture off a friend, a box of 12 bottles of red wine, would be the catalyst that would lead to traumatic events, not just for myself but for innocent persons caught up in my freefall of despair.

From the Good Friday to the evening of the proceeding Bank Holiday Monday, I would drink myself and take cocaine solidly in all that duration to the point of total psychosis, with no other fluids for three days except red wine and vodka coupled with the only solid to enter my body being cocaine up my nose, my delusions became perfectly real, my hallucinations vivid and my orientations totally inept.

Thoughts now engulfed me that an attempt on my life was moments away, with no shoes on, I fled the house where I had been throughout my gluttonous drug and alcohol binge.

To where and who I was fleeing from, only my deluded mind at that time could fathom that out; what I can remember in this positively psychotic state is very much a blur.

The running through hotel corridors on the Albert Dock Complex in Liverpool, through the docks complex itself, on top of the roof of vans, trying to navigate over high fences, hijacking terrified hackney cabs, eventually trying to orientate myself back to where I had come from.

Thinking I was at the same starting point of my terrified running spree, I jumped over the fences of a row of houses, that to me was the one I originally ran away from, but was where now that I sought refuge at, because now somebody was chasing me, as the laser sight of a gun tried to get a fix on my body.

With this I punched through a double-glazed window, slicing my wrist open. As I climbed through the window, I landed on the broken glass on the floor, cutting my leg open, exposing my knee cap. With the force of the fall, I also bit my tongue, severing it to a point it hung out my mouth like a tired bloodhound.

To escape the gun man, or gun men, I presumed there was more than one down to me hearing conversations amongst them as I smashed my way to safety, I headed up the stairs of the house, what I thought was the house I left 25 or so minutes previously, barricading myself in one of the upstairs rooms, I heard the running up the stairs of many.

With this, they tried to prise the door open, as again the red laser beam of a gun tried to get a fix on my body, I was now fighting for my life against a gang of would-be assassins.

Psychosis was complete, the reality was that I was not in the house where I started my rampage, I was in the house of an innocent person terrified and oblivious to what was happening, and the men with guns, well, I was correct about the men with guns, but they were not hitmen, far from it, they were the police, the laser light, was a gun getting pointed at me, it was a taser gun.

Eventually, after a long struggle to restrain me, secured with leather restraints of a stretcher, I was taken to the hospital. What I can remember, the doors of the ambulance opened and a team of hospital personnel were waiting for my arrival.

Receiving oxygen with a severed piece of my tongue hanging from my mouth, they began to stitch up the lacerations inflicted by my delusional state of mind. The wounds were very much real, as my exposed bone of the knee was closed over again, wrists and knuckles sealed tight, with the added consultation from a plastic surgeon over my hanging dog-like tongue, x-rays to legs and hands, I was then sent to a ward under police guard.

After languishing in hospital and a police cell for the next couple of days, a picture was being formed by the police over the circumstances leading up to my psychotic rampage and my past mental health issues, a sympathetic sergeant reassured me considering the circumstances now understood by themselves that he would try and get me home as soon as.

The Crime Prosecution Service didn't have the same sympathetic understanding. A court appearance was inevitable that same day in which a magistrate would deem me a threat to the public and myself, who in turn remanded me in custody to HMP Liverpool.

Arriving through the gates of the prison, passing the stringent security checks, the high walls topped with razor wire, was my first realisation I wasn't going anywhere in the immediate future. Booked in, as they called it, my name replaced by a number, my new standard uniform of an inmate put on, I was sent to be checked over by the doctor.

My injuries making me only just able to walk with a dragging limp, my speech impaired by my semi-detached tongue, the on-duty doctor came to the conclusion that my injuries having already been dealt with by the hospital, I was fit to be integrated into the normal prison system.

Worryingly, at no point was my mental health addressed in the analysis of myself, not even to the extent of asking how the lacerations to my wrist came about.

My first night would be spent in the wing for new admissions, my cell mate, a young gang member, whose chosen career path was to destroy cash machines with a piece of heavy-duty plant equipment, with the idea to extract the milk from the hard shell of this reinforced metal coconut, with the help and assistance from his also stolen mechanical digger.

The cell itself was quite fitting I suppose for someone who had broken the laws of the land. I wasn't expecting the Hilton. The wafer-thin mattress, the itchy blankets, graffiti-etched walls, and to round it off, a leaking toilet from the completely brown toilet bowl, there was no indication this toilet had been made of or exhibited the usual white porcelain of a standard bathroom piece.

The morning presented me with my first confrontation, an inmate who after using the showering facilities, thought I had infiltrated his money-making stash of drugs, with a commanding request to stay where I was. He ran up to the first landing where my appointed Her Majesty's temporary living quarters was.

Clutching a rolled-up towel, he asked if I had moved his consignment of contraband in a not-so-happy tone of voice. With this, thinking ahead, I gazed at the net over my balcony to stop the fall of flying inmates. I planned his flight path in my head quickly.

With my equally aggressive return in answering him, he then backed down, ran upstairs to the above landing, on which I heard the scuffle of two peeved individuals' heated discussion accelerate into more than just a heated exchange. The antagonist, rolled up in his towel was a chair leg, now not for the purpose to steadily sustain the balance and wait of a table top, was now used in hitting the person in the cell that he had pinpointed for his impromptu inspection.

Not backing down, the occupant quite willingly exchanged blows, the fracas was dealt with eventually by the prison officers, and the whole wing was placed on lockdown for the next 24 hours.

The next morning would see me assigned to my place of residence for the duration of my stay, my cellmate a Polish national, intelligent, conversation interesting, I had touched lucky with my co inhabitant.

The goings-on in a typical day, if you did not have a workplace to go to in the secure compound, was mundane to say the least. Near enough every day the old steel door would only open for you to go and receive your morning and evening meal so you could then take it back to your cell to feast upon.

The total time you would be secured in the small outdated Victorian cell would amount to 23 hours of your day; again, not to moan, these conditions should no way mirror the adequate setting of a travel lodge stay, and indeed they certainly didn't. They did however serve the purpose; again, I reiterate for somebody who finds themself in a brush with the law.

The exercise yard I had the chance to frequent just the once, every time I would head to the squared walking space, the doors would close, always down to inadequate staffing levels.

The prison wardens themselves, I must say, I had never met such a bunch of disillusioned, running-down-the-clock-of-their-shift workplace personnel in my entire life. Who could blame them, the abuse they would be subject to from inmates was in some cases despicable.

The landings were being controlled by the inmates. In some conversations I had, inmates had purposely landed themselves inside, so they could earn large amounts of money from selling drugs of all descriptions. The previous inmate of my cell, who was moved because of such antics, was reportedly earning in excess of £200 a day from the cell, with also being able to fund his own crack addiction in addition to his monetary gain.

This made perfect sense to me, every time my cell door was opened, I had a queue of inmates popping their heads in for his services, not realising that his shop had been closed and himself relocated.

On one evening, my cell mate gave out an all-mighty scream from our en-suite toilet, at least slopping out had been abolished on our block, his high-pitched vocal call was down to a visitor he had an encounter with in our bathroom.

The intruder came in the shape of a cockroach the size of which would not have looked out of place in the jungle of *I'm a Celebrity, Get Me Out of Here!* Of course in our situation, *I'm an Inmate, Get Me Out of Here!* didn't hold much wait unfortunately. With that we had to accept our oversized co inhabitations. There was no way we could call 'Rent a Kill', so accepting them as our crawly little pets was the best approach.

My friend from Poland now introduced me to the prison library, in turn opening my eyes and mind to a plethora of information and learning I had not really took advantage of at all since I was the member of the local library when I was a child, but had to boycott duly because of a £15 fine imposed on my mum and dad due to late returns in the late seventies. This was quite a sum of money to find, so boycotting the premises was the only way to avoid the pending charges.

After just over three weeks on remand with two court sessions in my absence, with the judge wanting more information on my mental health and all the circumstances to my arrest, my request for bail in front of the judge had arrived.

Before awaiting transportation to the court. A rigorous searching process had to be confronted.

The search that was going to be undertaken on me was going to be with one of the prison officers I had encountered in the visiting hall. To say he had a distaste for all the inmates was an under-statement.

With instructions for me to strip naked in one of the cubicles so he could visually conduct his search, I obeyed his command, with just my boxer shorts left around the ankle of one foot, I stood with arms outstretched, naked.

With now another more irate command coming from the officer in charge, he aggressively instructed me, "SHAKE!"

"I beg your pardon?" I replied.

His impatient return was again, "SHAKE!"

With this I began to shake my whole body, in particular my backside, from an unbiased take of my movement, it would have mirrored me trying to perform the popular dance move of the sixties, The Twist.

With the non-specific instruction, I shook and shimmied to the best of my ability, hopefully satisfying the prison officer's wish.

With a raging red face, the very overweight, high-blood-pressured prison officer bellowed out, "Not you, you fucking idiot, your boxer shorts from around your ankle, shake them off your foot!"

With my impromptu dance routine halted, I was told to wait in a holding room to await transport for my day of judgement.

Arriving at the Crown Court, three other inmates awaiting their appearance in front of the judge were put in the same holding cell as myself, as discussions of how their period of incarceration had treated them, one of the inmates quite calmly, so as not to interrupt the flow of the conversation, reached into his pocket, retrieved something unknown as yet to everyone else in the cell.

He then proceeded to undo his tiny wrapped-up sweetie, a Strepsil, maybe or Werther's Original – not quite – with clenched teeth around the housing of the object, he bit and spat out a small plastic knot, landing just short of my shiny polished court appearance best shoes.

He then, on the hard benched surface, put out a formidable amount of what I knew now was cocaine into a line, leaned over with a rolled-up piece of paper and undertook the delivery of the class A substance up his nostrils.

Astonished at his sheer calmness with also the non-bat of an eye lid reaction from the other awaiting court-appearing subjects, the conversation just carried on as if he had just sneezed momentarily, slightly unbalancing the flow of chit chat.

The magnitude of the absurdity was beyond my comprehension. I had seen everything now, a prison inmate coming from HMP, waiting for his turn in front a Crown Court judge, in a holding cell, openly snorting cocaine, a class A controlled drug, literally three feet away from a guard and police personnel.

To this day, I still cannot rationalise that day in the holding cell. I still find myself shaking my head in disbelief, when really it needs to join the back of the queue of the things I need to rationalise first in my life maybe.

Before my bail application was addressed, I had time to speak to a lady mental health social worker named Helen who was in attendance at the police station on my arrest. I explained I was actually thankful for my incarceration by the magistrate, with time to reflect, I totally deserved it in what my deluded state drove me to do.

The realisation that I did need saving from myself, taken back by my honesty, Helen relayed this to the judge, coupled with the evidence gathered by my wife regarding my past mental health battles, my charity work, evidence of proof of my character no solicitor could've sourced, it was down to my wife to present a steadfast case for a successful bail application.

My wife again had come to my rescue to make sure they had a true picture of the person I was. With no objections, I was granted bail pending another appearance in Crown Court regarding my punishment, in which more time in prison was not ruled out.

On the judge's, decision I looked at Helen in the witness box across the court room and said a heartfelt "thank you". Lip reading my gratefulness, I lip read her reply of "no problem" and a smile. The emotions and relief from my wife, daughter and of course myself on being reunited with them in the foyer of the Crown Court, is a moment I won't forget, but I do want to forget if that makes sense, putting them through another calamitous ordeal was just not fair on them but still, like countless times before, they had forsaken my atrocious actions and stood by me.

On release, I made an appointment with my GP, to yet again try and reach out for the help that I most urgently needed. My wife attended with me on the day of the appointment.

Explaining my predicament to the GP in attendance, I was frustratingly given the wrong advise yet again, handing me over an information card of the local alcohol anonymous meetings. My frustration boiled over, screwing it up and throwing it back rudely, but enough was enough, I was willing to take the steps to seek better mental health but at the same time I was lost in the desert of mental health with the drought of information and help regarding the subject.

Again, the help and support was from family, the structure of recovery again proven methods, once more a focus, once more the natural protagonists for the happiness secreting hormone serotonin, my dogs, running with them in the openness of fields, the wooded trails and streams.

This particular regime began at the start of the trees blossoming, clusters of bluebells giving a welcome colouring to the weather-worn ground the winter had created, daffodils standing tall and fresh inspecting the surroundings of their perennial appearance, the glimpses of new life from the undergrowth as creatures of the forest explored their new world, a new world of hazards. My world was full of the same hazards, hazards and pitfalls I had to keep in check for longer periods of time than I had in the past.

Chapter Nineteen
Marathon in London, Stabbed in Portugal, Arnold in Madrid.

My awareness of there not being much awareness regarding the plights of people with mental health issues, prompted me to focus on running the London Marathon for the mental health charity Mind. With this now in place and a place in London guaranteed through the charity themself, it would give me from getting released from prison about 11 months to prepare diligently, that was if I never received a jail sentence from the up-and-coming court appearance.

With all the evidence gathered regarding the causes of my mental health issues, my three appearances in the witness box as a pivotal witness in three murder trials, my previous good character, charity work and glowing character references from teachers, businessmen and the parents of critically-ill children who I had supported, the judge saw the appropriate sentence being a suspended two-year jail term, again to serve a period of time on house arrest, with also the understanding to receive treatment and help with my injuries to my mental state.

The latter bit of advice would still be an incredibly difficult area to infiltrate. Medication was recommended, which I reluctantly tried. Meetings with a psychiatrist were put in place; on attending these one-to-one sessions, again I would find the root causes were not being addressed, instead a generic approach for diagnosis and recovery was being applied, one method for everyone, no individual assessment results or on hearing my specific story, I just didn't see what this treatment had to offer. My proven methods of rehabilitation were paying massive dividends again, I just needed a plan to sustain stability from my initial starting of rehab, as long as other out-of-the-ordinary episodes never arose again.

My day running the streets of London came around in the April of 2015, cheered on by my family, my hard work paid off massively, the experience of over thirty years making mistakes in training, correcting them, nutrition a key to all sports people, I had perfected after the years of weight training for bodybuilding shows, dropping five stone in body weight, hitting the scales on race day at 14 stone 6 pounds.

With again my family cheering my every step, there they were, at the 13.1 halfway stage as promised, at the precise time I said I would be, the charity Mind who I was running on behalf of, providing a front-row vantage point for high fives as I swiftly passed them.

Somehow they found themselves at the 23-mile marker as well. Again the much-needed encouragement I embraced into every sinew of tired muscle to get myself across the finishing line.

From being morbidly obese at 19st 2lbs with a mind just as obese with broken thoughts just 16 months previously, I broke my personal best marathon time clocked some 18 years previously in New York; at the age of 45, I crossed the tape in 3 hours 34 minutes.

On the home straight, Buckingham Palace came into view, turning onto the Mall, a welling up of my eyes blurred the bright red sponsor's name across the finish.

An immense sense of privilege, an immense feeling of thankfulness for my family who had stood by me, just 12 months back I was languishing in a prison cell, beaten, battered in mind and in body, but with a direct approach and a willingness, I faced up to my frailties, the music emitting from my headphones calculated perfectly for the home straight, *Land of Hope and Glory*.

On finishing, thousands of pounds had been raised for the mental health charity Mind and an awareness of the subject to top it off.

Nearly a year now had passed since I was released from prison, things were good, mentally very good. So good was my progress, the mental health social worker Helen who was instrumental in my successful bail application, gave me an opportunity to speak about my experiences down in London's Canary Wharf, at a conference with people from around the country with similar experiences. She also nominated myself for a national award for inmates of the prison system who had turned their circumstances around, missing out on the accolade but nevertheless to be nominated was a real boost to my mental defences.

Physically, I was starting to exhibit lean muscle tissue not shown on my skeleton for a long time; such was the difference, I was willing to step on a stage for judgement of my physique, but not in any serious competitive realm, but to bring awareness of mental health, this time wearing board shorts in the same show that I had entered 25 years previous, winning the junior under-21 bodybuilding category, this time in the over-40s physique class.

After doing the show in a spur-of-the-moment decision, with the likening of being on stage again, I made plans to try and home in on my diet more precisely. It also kept my focus inline, so I planned a competition to do at the NEC in Birmingham: The BodyPower Expo.

The class of over-40s is who I would try and mix it up with, a beach bodied appearance, not too heavily muscled, coupled with the not-as-ripped-as-a-bodybuilder's physique, was the vague criteria and the desired look for the physique classes.

My participation in Birmingham on the Saturday would be part of a weekend that would include a half marathon attempt in Chester on the Sunday less than 24 hours after being on stage for the physique contest.

I would notch up a credible 4th placing in Birmingham. The Chester half marathon I would excel in, bursting through the tape in the centre of the old historic Roman town, equalling my own personal best again 18 years previously, in a time of just over 1 hour 30 minutes, at a very lean body weight of 14 stone 6 pounds.

More significantly, more astonishingly, was for over a year now, I had no serious bouts of depression, well, not to be serious enough to make them disrupting to render me what I would class as immobile.

My none too serious approach to physique contests would take me to different parts of the country. I was in a contest within myself not with any other person, a fight in fact, one in which at that moment in time, I was delivering competition to, and winning unanimously. One such competition, given the glamorous name of the English Grand Prix, I would decide to participate in. My stage endeavours on this occasion would see me take second place to the current British Champion at the time, but it also would give me the chance to fulfil another ambition, to compete on stage abroad, with an invitation for recognition of a second-place podium finish – The Arnold Classic Expo in Madrid would be my next port of call in the competitive stakes.

I had competed abroad in road races before, my last one in the March of 2015, a race stretching over the Italian and French Riviera finishing at the harbour area of Monaco in the Riviera Classic.

On this occasion after the race, enjoying lunch in my hotel with my wife, a resident of Monaco would also be in attendance with her family, a legend and sporting hero of mine, Dame Paula Radcliffe, posing for a photo with me, we swapped future plans of racing.

It was just so that she was participating in the London Marathon that year as well, her farewell race, having already shared the same race with her in New York in 2007, which she was the victor of in the women's race, it would be great to say I was in that last marathon of this fabulous athlete, and person might I add, Dame Paula Radcliffe.

Before the rigours of dieting took a hold, me and family would do our usual trip over to Portugal, where every year we would take our daughter to celebrate her birthday. This year would be no different. I had seven weeks to prepare for my somewhat surprising stage outing at The Arnold Classic Madrid, so off we went to Portugal, Vilamoura to be precise in the Algarve.

Jollities ensued on the opening night of our holiday, a meal in our favourite marina restaurant, followed by drinks at a bar favoured by golfers on the same marina.

A heavy presence of club-goers entering the resort was noticed on the surrounding roads of the resort, all headed in the direction of our hotel again on the marina.

Having met up with long-time friends from Liverpool who also had attended my gym for the past 30 years, the night drew to an end. My wife, daughter and friends decided to retire to the comfort of their rooms while me and the boyfriend of my daughter at the time decided to follow the crowd who were heading in the direction of our hotel anyway.

Another entrance to the hotel presented itself at the far end of where we would've entered normally. The entrance we happily strolled into was the entrance to a section of the hotel that was used to hold events such as the one that was happening this evening in question.

As we strolled up to the front door, we had the idea that after we had satisfied our curiosity on what was happening, we could just cut through the event and straight into our hotel. A large line of people to the left of us presented itself as we turned the corner from the right, with this we headed up to the entrance.

A gentleman small in stature, in a suit, was our point of reference to ask could we cut in through the entrance into the hotel, which we were residents of. Not speaking any English, he held the palm of his hand out in a rather military style halt. On trying to explain our intention, he clicked his fingers towards one of many security personnel around him.

With this, a burly, black-tied, black-suited human guard dog was commanded by his owner by a click of his fingers, let off his leash with a lolloping type of movement over to me. Obeying his master, he greeted me with not a bite but with a feeble punch to the nose that certainly had the purpose of trying to render me unconscious had it of been thrown by a more competent pugilist.

Brushing the punch off with more a startled surprise than of any hurt, I asked the question what the hell was that for. With this, three other men in black came from the rear, with their surprise cowardly attack struck my companion on the head, felling him unconscious on the shiny tiled floor.

As I moved myself to a more defendable position, I was outnumbered at this point by five to one. The next wave of attack was by one of the personally handpicked by the master on the front entrance, as again he gave instructions to this smaller, stockier figure to attack, launching two side-kicks to my legs with the intention of bringing me down to the floor.

I realised by the favouritism showed by the master this was their ace in the pack, to be fair, very capable indeed to inflict injury to myself, with well-honed skills of kicking, he was surely a practitioner in some sort of martial arts.

My instinct of pugilism and its lead hand stance rammed two not-so-accurate left-hand jabs to his face, brushing his shoulder as he pulled back defensively. Another kick landed flush on the side of my leg, nearly sweeping my feet from under me; countering with a one two, I caught the over-confident assailant on the cheek. A retreat and a second thought was assessed by my foe.

As I adjusted my footing, a bottle was smashed down on top of my head, the spraying of glass an indication of the force of the blow. A glance back quickly, the guilty party a tall long-haired man, again all dressed in the code of black, he backed off. Quickly turning my focus back to the front of me, my one-to-one situation had now tripled.

Now outnumbered by seven to one, I knew I was in serious trouble. The three from the front closed in with at least two from the rear of me jumping on my back. A choke hold was put around my neck as I tried to guide my teeth to the hands of the vice-like hold as elbows, punches and kicks rained down onto my face and body.

Then a sharp pain to my neck, with it the sound of ripping cloth, but this wasn't my t-shirt being ripped in the fracas, this was my neck being opened up by a wafer-thin piece of steel of a knife. The close proximity of my ears to the slashing was the sound of my skin tearing open, not the polyester combination that my t-shirt was comprised of.

The zig-zagging motion of the cowardly thug's wrist actions created a Zorro-like engraved signature wound to my neck. The warmth of my own blood saturated the whole rear of my body down to my lower back.

I tried in a last-ditch attempt to pull the pack of cowardly thugs down with me as my fading consciousness overwhelmed my now exhausted fight.

A rifling of my body ensued as they stripped me of anything worth taking from my pockets and around my wrist, which included a 40th birthday present from my wife, in the form of a very expensive time-piece – the worth was for me all in a sentimental way – my smart phone and wallet with the housed contents of cash and cards also pilfered in their mugging act.

The next thing I could remember was being lifted up and with a brief momentarily weightlessness, I was thrown towards the water of the marina, landing in a heap just short of the rocky drop into the briny drink, then darkness.

A strong light shone into my eyes, with an overwhelming pain, a pain I had never ever encountered before was in my side, the same to my neck, an indescribable tugging, a searing, intense pain.

The lights were the lights of the operation theatre in Faro Hospital, surgeons stitched up my open wounds to my neck, hip and arm with no anaesthetic, hence the insufferable pain, my injuries caused by, from what the doctors said, the clinical sharpness of a scalpel.

Such an implement only generally used in an operation theatre by a surgeon, the other possibility was an unused razor, more worryingly was how close the blade was away from cutting through a main artery, the consultant surgeon revealed it to be in millimetres.

Nose broke with the persistent use of elbows thrust into it, knees, feet and arms grazed, down to my impromptu flight towards the depths of the marina. I resided in intensive care attached to drips, with my only thoughts being I can't miss my daughter's birthday celebrations that night.

No way were a group of cowardly, bullying thieves from the now-demolished Seven Club that was attached to our hotel on the marina, going to stop me from attending my daughter's birthday, which was that same day.

With this incentive of my daughter's birthday, I relayed my wishes to the attending nurses; my proposal was somewhat smirked at, in the fact I was going nowhere. My mind made up, I dressed myself with the help of my wife and daughter, pulling my fresh clothes over my Egyptian mummy head of bandages.

I hobbled towards the exit, with it a nurse quickly walking and shouting to me in Portuguese holding the paper work of self-discharging, with the added recommendation of I couldn't leave with the drip I was dragging with me on wheels still attached to my arm, which I totally forgot about due to my sheer determination to exit the building.

The extent of the men in black's cowardly attack upon myself became clear on returning back to my hotel room. Their pack mentality of aggression exhibited that of a frenzied animal attack as I reflected on what they had done and the resulting injuries.

The cowardly attack personified by the Z-like scar to the back of my neck, attacking someone from behind with a knife undoubtedly showed the character of the assailant, a shithouse, sorry for the language, but I struggled for the appropriate descriptive word; the one used was the most fitting.

I made my daughter's birthday meal, a slightly subdued affair understandably, but I made it, alive.

Statements made to the reluctant police force the next day, made it clear to me it would be a fruitless attempt for justice, their attitude non-enthusiastic, and with the supposedly attempt to recover the CCTV footage that would have caught the whole incident clear as day by the sophisticated cameras, suspiciously going missing, a collaborated cover-up was certainly evident.

After leaving the police station, me and my family headed to the marina for dinner. Not having any particular restaurant singled out, we hovered outside one scanning the menu, when a young waiter came running over to me shouting, "Our hero, look, our hero is here!"

Bemused with his comments, I looked around to see who he was suggesting was the hero; it was me. With a two-handed grasp of my shoulders, he started thanking me. What for, I questioned.

He then went on to tell me how I had stood up to the notorious bullying cowards of the Seven Club, apparently giving the bunch of all-in-black-tailored suits men a run for their money., My resulting injuries did not suggest that at any point I was in the running for anything except a severe beating.

They continued detailing the antics of them beating up kids and subsequently robbing them. They were renowned all over the area for it, especially at this particular spot on the marina.

Witnessing what they had done to me, they were only too willing to help the police with their inquiries, a court appearance if necessary as well. They even pinpointed the knife attacker, the long-haired, tall figure who had made me feel the glass bottle on top of my head, the guilty party, again renowned for this type of assault on somebody he knew was not in a position to defend themselves or fight back.

The joy of all the young waiters heralded us a sought-after privileged table in the restaurant as their guests, a warming gesture from the true people of Portugal, where me and my family continue to holiday to this day. As for the renowned Seven Club, demolished, a reputation the high-starred hotel couldn't carry any longer due to the list of growing incidents from the ugly establishment that once adjoined them.

Seven was also the time duration in weeks, in which I had to train and diet rigorously, that's if I was in the best of health to start with, of course that was far from the condition I was in returning home.

My first appointment on home soil was at the local hospital. Attention had to be paid to the way the Portuguese surgeon had sewn up my neck. It turned out it was not the best bit of crocheting skills in the world, which had left a tongue-like piece of skin protruding out of the end of the Z-like wound to my neck.

The towel was about to be thrown in when I was in the hospital bed in Faro.

"Well, that's Madrid down the sink," I conceded in a tone of defeat.

Had it not been for my wife and daughter's encouragement that I had plenty of time to recover if I applied the same resilience towards my goal of stepping on stage in Madrid at The Arnold Classic that I had in other times of adversity, Madrid would still be a possibility.

My running was still a pivotal part of my self-preservation and of course my Boston pack needed their daily dose of frolics. With feet still swollen, with the grated parts of my knees and legs still in the early stages of new skin growth, the cracking of the freshly-formed scabs brought more discomfort to my new injury adjusted style of running.

This was a minor cross to bear. Slight seeping dark cracks started to appear in my mind, due to the few days only literally of no activity, putting up with the aches, pains and the stinging effects of sweat running into my fresh wounds was nothing compared to the torturing injuries of the mind I would suffer if I didn't squeeze my injured feet into my trail-adapted running shoes.

My family's assumptions of recovery were correct as the external injuries started to heal satisfyingly quickly. My internal injuries also abated. Surprisingly, The Arnold Classic was now again very much on the cards.

Breathing in the atmosphere of this huge event, the biggest of its kind in Europe, competitors milled around the halls of the expo, gaunt-looking in the face due to the rigours of dieting, and I was one of them, I had made it.

The fast healing process of my body renewing severed tissue and scraped skin, was ample enough for me make the journey over to the capital of Spain.

Soaking up this unique experience, chatting to people from all over Europe, browsing around the innovative fitness products, equipment and get-fit fads of the dreamy entrepreneur, all about to hit their respective marketplace, was truly mentally inspiring moment.

Taking my daily dose of medication early every morning, running around the still half-asleep city, I felt invigorated, rejuvenated, again without the pressure the other competitors were putting on themselves over competition, I had already won my personal mini battle by just being able to attend.

The buzz of the vast multi-staged events hall had another unique buzz about it the first day, the arrival of its patron, Arnold Schwarzenegger.

Crowds swarmed around the stage where he was speaking, in awe of their hero who portrayed the cyborg that was *The Terminator*. At one point over the weekend, I would see Arnold himself give an impromptu performance as the conductor of an orchestra at the event, giving his battened hand waving gesture timings to the theme of *The Terminator* films, a strange viewing it was, I must say.

The competition itself, I had the honour of leading out the line-up to the over-40s men's physique class., I lapped up the experience in front of my family and the hundreds of people in attendance watching our class, just being able to step on stage after the awful events in Portugal, I had beat my inner tormentors again, for now anyway.

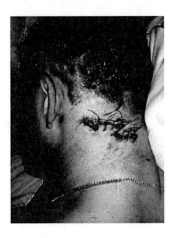

The knife wound to my neck suffered after being attacked and robbed on a family holiday in Portugal

Just seven weeks after the incident in Portugal outside the auditorium in Madrid ready to compete at the Arnold Classic Europe

Running the London Marathon for the mental health charity MIND in 2015

Chapter Twenty
Drastic Action Taken and Not Taken

With another five weeks of focus on training and diet for the purpose of the steady flow of serotonin that my chosen form of medication provided, I continued with my proven methods. An end of the competitive season at the British Championships was the target, at the end of the five weeks was the precise goal, but a new persistent problem kept arising: my knees which had carried me around five boroughs of New York twice, London and Rotterdam running from at top weight of 17 stone 3 pounds, were showing signs of wear and tear. My own medication was bearing signs of side-effects. At this point though, not enough to disrupt my daily dosed application.

After the latest regimented period came to an end, listening to people say, you need a rest, you're going to burn yourself out, I lost my way of thinking of why I was doing this strict disciplined way of life. It wasn't for my physical well-being or appearance, that was just a by-product, my mental well-being was the purpose. People just saw the rigours of my training regime that to them was outrageous, but to me was the way I kept my stability mentally. Under a wave of the same advice, my guard dropped, virtually instantly the decline started, going to work again would pose the same apparitions in my mind when I would cross the threshold of the gym, the same dreadful visions, the same disastrous antidotes would resurface.

Facts and reality had to be faced. I was clinging on to a place I had grown up in since the age of thirteen; I was now forty six years of age. Times had changed. It was the only thing I knew, but it was also the main reminder of what was causing my mental discontent. A major decision, a major change in direction had to be made, with it a huge gamble, but there was also a huge gamble staying. I had to be brave and walk away and don't look back, ever.

Before I switched off the last remaining light in the gym, I picked up a hardwood sign with the original name of the gym engraved into the wood, the sign a gift from a member who I also classed as a friend as well, who in fact was tragically killed in a road traffic accident, this was the only reminder I took on the night I gave the place I spent most of my life in one last look, it was my life, cherished memories, heinous times, filtering out the good and bad of the both in my mind, was the task I found most difficult. The door locked, I walked away, not looking back once, as not to encourage second thoughts of emotion.

With a knowing now I had erased a formidable obstacle, or more of an antagonist to my struggles mentally, even if it was a huge decision, a life-changing move for the better health wise, it was the right move nonetheless. The radical change also freed up time during the evenings due to late shift work that I had grew up with. This opportunity presented me with a chance to take up again my first sporting passion, boxing.

This would also add another scaffold frame around my thoughts, to channel and focus my mind into my new pastime, with the also convenient resting of my now continually swollen and painful knees from the long runs preparing for hard surface road races which played havoc with my joints of the leg.

The atmosphere of this type of gym I had missed since being a really young boy, the energy and the enthusiasm from the young boxers, male and female, was contagious and respectful for their new gym mate who was more than double their age in myself.

My fitness levels though from this old timer, would make it possible for me to keep up with youngsters, most being younger than my own children.

Mentally strong and thriving with the challenge of being in the squared ring, a competitive bout was singled out, again having the added incentive of raising money for a cause close to me. Raising money for charity was always a mental strength solidifier for myself during my marathon days. This would be no exception and it just so happened friends of mine were in the process of raising money for an operation for their daughter who had cerebral palsy. This would be my personal worthwhile incentive to face the punches of competition.

At this point in time, my runs accompanied by my usual Boston running partners, would have to be initially undertaken on soft ground, an added cushion for my now crumbling knees, with the vision of the early rising of the sun over the woodlands, as the golden shine would hit the summit of the towering old oaks, as me and my pack would amble along, joyfully swimming in the pools of serotonin, not at all disrupted by my now tentative running gate.

Fight week was intense, adrenaline brimming. Like a coiled spring, I just wanted the first bell to ring. The weigh-in produced again a slimmed down me, to the weight of 14 stone 4 pounds, inside the limit of the cruiserweight division. My opponent would be from Manchester, exactly half my age at 23, and with a more active experience in the ring.

A strange attitude, or should I say a non-concern of being punched to the head and body I found had embodied myself. My reasoning for this was down to my struggles with my mental hurting that I carried around constantly; to get hit by a punch momentarily was nothing compared to the unforgiving irrational combination barrages of thought I was accustomed too.

What was also interesting with training and mixing with the young boxers, was that some of them also suffered troubling mental thoughts. With this form of training, the collective narrative was that it was a huge boost to the fragilities of their mental processing. I could now testify once a session of sparring was complete the mutual respect for your opposite number, not just of admiration, there was a sense of accomplishment. The by-product then was a bolstering effect to your state of mind in confidence and an uplifting of your mood, instantly.

The anticipation of combat channelled the right way with a dusting of nerves because of the very real threat of being hurt. I had found the right proportions within myself, climbing through the ropes alone was a feeling I was accustomed to due to my loneliness of covering up my fight within myself.

With the bell ringing, my natural laid-back pleasant nature had to be put to one side immediately, as my opponent ran at me as if he wanted to dislodge my head from its perch on top of my shoulders; after all, this wasn't a tickling competition, adjusting my train of thought to the job in front of me.

I started to work behind my left-hand jab, keeping my hands up and being first to the punch. This advice I received as a schoolboy, the advice basic, but fundamentally as accurate as you could ever wish for to take into the fisticuffs of competition.

But this advice I carry around today to warn me about myself, to work behind a positive attitude, to keep my guard up for negativities and to act first on detection of such threats; the fundamentals of combat are the same for the fight with yourself internally.

With the intervening of the dickie-bowed officiate in the third round, a TKO victory was recorded for me. The admiration from myself and my opponent between us both after it was waved off, was a pleasant feeling of good sportsmanship. My hand being raised as the victor against an opponent half my age was huge to my morale of good mental longevity. Like my on-stage antics of the physique world, I wanted more, not just for the competition but for the structure, the discipline and the subsequent steady streaming of serotonin.

A successful fundraising campaign would also be another win raising around the £1500 mark for my friend's daughter's much-needed operation. Eight weeks later, I would again climb through the ropes, this time the recruitment of a long-time friend, Michael Carr, to fight on behalf of my friend's daughter as well, in which his efforts topped £2000. Both of us that night came away with points wins, the main winner being my friend's little daughter who went on to have her operation with the help of our combined efforts in the ring and the contributions from our supporters.

The next few months, my troublesome knees would limit my running excursions to short durations, at a pace some would determine as a brisk walk. The pain and inflammation was now unbearable, the swelling unsightly as my joints of the leg would become a lot bigger in circumference than that of my thighs.

My boxing training would also be hindered; with no acute bending of the knees, certain training drills would be a no-go. Even in sparring, a slight twist to either leg and they would totally give way. After two more fights, one being with my opponent only being 18 years of age, a 23-year age gap, so in the October of 2017 after a sparse amount of training that was dictated by my now severe patella problems, I was scheduled to fight again, the battle in front of me now leading up to the fight was three-pronged, my opponent who I knew and very capable, my now not as strong mental state due to the inactivity forced by injuries and the agonising pain from my knees.

Fight night, the will to put up my dukes was still as strong as ever, in fact it felt strangely like it was a safe haven calling, but first a medical that every boxer took on the night of the bout. Not worried at all by this examination, I had recorded better readings than some of my younger counterparts in my last fights, in fact in one contest in Birmingham against an opponent who was 18 years of age, a 28-year age difference, my ops were not that far away from his, this time I was in for a major shocker.

This would be my first TKO against myself, but it wouldn't come way of the third man in the ring, it would come from the officiates from the health examination even before a punch had been thrown.

My observations took by the paramedic in attendance, was cause for major concern. It was my blood pressure; my systolic reading was hovering in the mid-190s and my diastolic was at a very concerning level as well. With the advice of the paramedic, I was told to find a quiet corner to sit for an hour or so to see if it would lower, suggesting it might just be pre-fight nerves contributing to the high readings.

The paramedic's suggestion bore no fruit. An hour later, my reading this time of asking was higher than the previous. With this, I was pulled out of the contest. The disappointment hit me hard, but the thought of another element health wise to deal with, was devastating to my now shaky mental state. On advice from the paramedic, his concern so high, he even suggested for me to go to A&E to get an ECG, or to certainly on the next available opportunity to go and see my GP.

Just because my guard wasn't needed that night in the ring due to the postponement of my bout, I should have still had my guard high outside the ring regarding my fragile mind, but alas I never did and sought solace in a bottle of Russian fire water, vodka. This in turn led to another old acquaintance, cocaine; with my reunion complete, so was my decline into mental despair.

On the brink of some sort of serious cardiac problem, risking a stroke or heart attack, I adopted the most outrageous behaviour by someone facing such serious health risks; I was literally playing Russian roulette with my existence.

The rope-a-dope tactic I employed was not to wear out my opponent with the plan to come on stronger when they had gassed out, my opponent was the formidable destroyer in the guise of mental illness. This opponent only grew in strength and would never lose momentum. I had given up the fight. With no one to throw in the towel, it was a slow progressive beating.

Over the next few weeks, there was a rapid decline with my mobility due to the worsening conditions of my knees. Walking just a few steps became excruciating. I was oblivious to my blood pressure readings after not following up the recommendations from the medics at the fight venue, total disregard for my health, for my life was at an all-time low. Sleep was my way of avoiding all detrimental thoughts. I had the ability to force my body into a slumbering state for most of a day's 24 hours, eventually even in my dreams my thoughts would catch up to me, turning my sleeping sanctuary into nightmares.

My own strategies to ward away tsunami thoughts of devastation had been withdrawn from me. My legs could not perform the work the same way an antidepressant prescription would have worked by running, or even just walking my dogs in the woods that would have in the past remedied the situation, but my thoughts would take me into the woods at the other end of the scale for the purpose of not to cure, but to end.

Chapter Twenty-One
Spiritual Intervention

The overwhelming invasion of thoughts of defeat against the negative powers that were now mental and physical, bombarding me constantly, with no let-up, a perfect storm was forming, a catastrophic system of thought was now totally out of control.

The process in my mind now was simple, the quickest way to stop this insufferable torture, a blinkered attitude now of planning the unthinkable to some, but to myself a perfectly reasonable solution to my predicament.

My plan now was hatching into my corrupt way of thought, with a calming demeanour, as resolute if I had just decided to go to the local convenience store, my journey to my singled-out resting point got under way.

My backpack equipped with the one necessary item to fulfil the purpose intended, a piece of gym equipment, suspension rings, the strong material of which was used to perform specific bodyweight exercises attached to a steel frame, their use on this dark wet winter's night in late November was not to strengthen the body or condition it, one end wrapped around the branch of a tree the other around my neck, on dropping from a strong enough branch, would cure the pain and silence the voices willing me on to perform the life-ending task.

The other essential part of the plan, my phone, in which for one hour before I trudged through the complete darkness of the wood, carefully detailed my reasonings behind my self-imposed cure to my illness, where I could be recovered from, the love I had for my family, individual messages to my wife and children, technical suicide notes once delivered by the pressing of a button, the trap door would open and the intended deed complete, on the sending of the said reasoning with information, there would no halting the self-inflicted execution.

My preferred gallows would be a strong tall oak in the middle of the ruins of an old building that used to house the priests from the nearby church, the remains of the old building only just visible now through the now heavily wooded area.

Navigation would be easy for myself in the near pitch black darkness of the night, it was part of my woodland trail runs which I had swiftly covered on numerous occasions with my pack of little Boston Terriers. Arriving at my destination, with no urgency, I unpacked the one-itemed content of my backpack. The necessary anchor point above me pinpointed. I proceeded to secure the suspension rings around the thick slippery bark of the old oak.

Everything in place, a definite attitude, now looking back at my disturbing calmness of acceptance to the task ahead, sent chills down my spine, but what would unravel next thankfully would not be the rolled-up nylon suspension rings placed next to me waiting for the gravity of the situation to render them taut.

With the final act of contact to my loved ones, I reached in my pocket for my high-tech smart phone; the first message retrieved that I composed earlier, my ice cold finger headed to the direction of the send button.

Only months old with no problem ever occurring from its intended use before, with a signalling strength at full bar, my mobile device suddenly blackened.

On the screen, in the middle a swirling circle appeared, as if it was trying to load data. My phone had been immobilised, turning on and off the device never erased the problem as this function had been made inoperable. The same rotating circle prevailed constantly, the use of the phone was impossible.

The sending of my final thoughts and wishes was impossible, there was no way I would leave this world without telling the people dear to me the reasoning behind my actions.

What happened next I can only describe as a warm inner glow of reassurance that things would get better. It wasn't my time type of feeling embodied me. With this I clambered down from my perch, a huge smile of comfort exploded across my face as I hurriedly packed away what I had only just moments precisely before erected, stuffing the backpack, not even zipping it up. I ran, not for one minute the pain in my knees relevant, laughing this time onto an open field, waterlogged with mud sucking my footwear down. I didn't care. A new lease of life had empowered me.

Drenched with the drizzle coming down from the heavens, I was drenched with the joy I was not ascending up to the heavens. A rummage around my tracksuit bottoms, I again took a glance at my non-functional mobile phone. To my astonishment, the screen showed its functionality to be once again normal, as my preferred screen-saver lit up my face and its immediate surroundings of the dark and windswept field.

The next day, invigorated, motivated, willing to find a cure to my aliments, appointments made to my GP regarding the issues of mobility and blood pressure and until these issues were addressed successfully, maybe medication for my mind, even though it had not worked in the past, my first appointment would take me to a healer of a different kind.

Still utterly taken aback at what had happened in the wood two days earlier, I took up the invite to attend the Liverpool Spiritualist Church. What would be told to me on this evening would totally convince me my actions two nights earlier were intercepted by energies not yet understood by myself yet. The explanations given to me at this meeting, this would in turn give me more defence against the negative forces of my mind.

Sat in the packed church near the back, the meeting addressed as an open circle gathering of mediums, not knowing what to expect, I sat listening intently to the gifted and the people in attendance who spiritually had been singled out by a medium with a message to be passed onto them.

After about halfway into the meeting, the lady who was heading the gathering, abruptly interrupted proceedings to direct her focus towards me.

"Could I just interrupt for a moment please?" as she stood up from her chair, "I am overwhelmingly drawn to you, sir. I have an older gentleman impatiently pacing up and down the aisle. He is very smartly dressed, in fact, immaculately presented."

Generally, in an open circle, this lady didn't get involved with the goings-on, it was left to the other open circle medium participants who were still trying to perfect their gift of being an intermediate for the spirits of people who had passed over, to relay messages to relatives and friends alike.

The person the messenger was in contact with after filtering her depictions of him was my granddad O'Brien. The description given was undeniably my always impeccably turned out Granddad, my mother's farther; old photographs would testify to his way of presenting himself in the best possible way.

Unfortunately, he was tragically killed by bank robbers in a hit and run long before I was born. His message that would be told to me by the head medium would make every hair on my body stand up. The term gobsmacked I would say was accurate to describe my reaction the information had on me.

"Do you understand what happened to your phone the other evening and why?"

I couldn't believe firstly what was being said to me, as I adjusted myself to rationalise the questioning, with my voice now barely able to respond due to the lump in my throat.

I answered, "Yes."

The medium then went on to say, "So you understand about the phone, it was done for a reason, that only you know why?"

With the message delivered, she smiled, I smiled back as the journey of a tear made its way south down my cheek.

Only I knew about my phone becoming inoperable that night in the wood. I also did know that there was a presence, a spiritual presence, protecting me that evening without a doubt, a spiritual power that relieved me of a torturing mindset that so very nearly overpowered me, the cementing of my belief because of the comforting words from beyond that is out of reach of our intellect to understand, was my guardian angel, if you like, who was looking out for me, intervening when necessary, my granddad O'Brien.

Remarkably, a few minutes later, a medium residing in the inner circle also honed in on my presence in the room. A greeting from a spirit by what was described as a friendly punch to the shoulder, by a tall dark handsome person roughly in his mid-thirties, wanting to say hello to me. The greeting described would be a common gesture of acknowledgement me and my best mate Rob would greet each other with. It became such a relaxing, comforting feeling knowing there were positive energies channelling towards me.

After the meeting concluded, the head medium who passed the message from my granddad made a bee-line towards me, apparently again such interactions were uncommon, embracing me with a sincere hug, and whispered in my ear, "I hope that helped you."

With that, she smiled a contented smile, as if she knew what the disruption to my phone had prevented.

You can indeed make your own conclusions to the circumstances, the happenings, whether coincidently timed or not, but what I took out of it was a determination of renewed will, optimism for the future regarding my mental and physical health, a catalyst to provide the initial shove in the right direction.

Chapter Twenty-Two
One Step at a Time

With a list of health problems now to address, I set out a plan of action of which to confront first. My blood pressure readings I knew could be confronted immediately, the appropriate action of medication, blood tests, ECGs etc., were taken care of. My knee problem tied in with my recovery from my mental health issues, knowing by seeking treatment was reassurance in itself that I was tackling the ailment hindering my progress mentally, literally until I knew the extent of my joint problems I self-contained myself with my dogs as the immediate medication I required.

This self-isolation with the unconditional love of my pack showed dividends almost straightaway, beginning with short walks into the same woodland I had trudged through on that dark November evening, it now held a much more jubilant rite of passage, the rite of way I had been accustomed to when circumnavigating the trails and paths for the purpose of beating PBs in road races, to optimise my fitness, or to limit my body fat accumulation for my other sporting pursuits.

Surprisingly, certain aspects of my inability to roam freely due to the state of play with my knees actually started to help me mentally. Driving became too precarious due to medication making me drowsy, with the operation of the vehicle, pushing down on pedals triggering sharp painful prods to my knees, I turned into a positive.

The now very limited borders of my capabilities of walking, was in fact a recalibrating of my mind as well. Not using a car eliminated getting irate with other not-so-diligent drivers, an added bonus, a calmer disposition prevailed, a lowering of blood pressure was also a benefit I contributed to my non-motorised way of mobility.

A realisation started to dawn on me when x-rays and MRI scan results on my knees showed irreversible conditions.

The conclusions from surgeons and experts in the field were drastic ones, it was to replace both knees, but the problem would again arise with the replacements themselves needing replacing after 15 years or so. In a nutshell, I was too young for such a procedure.

A plan of maxing out what was left with my knees was put in place. A minor operation to trim what meniscus cartilage I had left, the torn and stretched ACL on both knees would have to be supported with non-surgical braces which would also straighten my now-bowed legs.

Both knees from tests also showed signs of different stages of arthritis, in certain parts exhibiting stage 4, the worst grade of the condition. This couldn't be cured but there were possible ways of relieving the pain caused by the condition. Unfortunately, injections of cortisone or taking any type of anti-inflammatory like Ibuprofen would be out of the question due to my acute hypertension. Relief of the daily pain was much needed though, but posed other problems in the form of addiction. Codeine would be a saint but if not used only intermittently or only when the pain was unbearable, could become a devilment of dependency.

By the end of 2018, all procedures had taken place. The operation to trim the sparse meniscus cartilage and a cleaning of inside the knee had taken place, braces were fitted to both legs, my now substituted ACLs in the form of the non-surgical braces were even given a run out in a 10k road race that me and my daughter completed on the Boxing Day of this year.

The full year of a dedication to resolve all the contributing factors to steady the sinking ship that was myself had been undertook, all because of the enlightened moment that late November evening, in the company of the tall old oak tree.

Going into the New Year should have been a time of steady progress that I had resigned myself to, with all the treatments showing signs of working, I would be mentally be tested in a different way like never before, with the past year progressively making the small step-by-step placements and strategies, a stronger mental reserve started to develop again. The timing of my more rigid and less fragile mental state would be much needed in the first few weeks of the new year.

My mother, Joan Elizabeth Scott, would be admitted into hospital at Aintree in Liverpool, the pillar of strength that supported me, who sat at my bedside as a child when sick or had a nightmare, who also sat at my beside as an adult when at my lowest living in a nightmare, who suffered in silence with her own mental frailties of depression for most of her life, was losing her battle now with what was diagnosed as pulmonary fibrosis.

At the end of three weeks in hospital, seeing this little lady give every last bit of fight against her condition, my father, myself and three brothers were given the heart-breaking news there was nothing more the doctors could do.

Gathered around her bedside with the doctor in attendance, he told my mother the severity of her condition, with the reassuring question to my mum the doctor asked, "Can we have your permission to make you more comfortable, Joan?"

Knowing what that really meant, taking it with the dignity and bravery I had accustomed my mother with all my life, my mother returned with her words of consent.

With the end-of-life procedures put into place, for the next three days her husband for the past fifty years and the three sons able to attend, paid vigil at her bedside, not leaving the hospital once, only leaving her beside momentarily in the whole seventy-two hours.

In this period of time, we played my mother's favourite recording artist, Elvis Aaron Presley, her favourite relaxing radio station, conversation wandered between my father and brothers of our cherished memories growing up, relaying them out loud so my mother in her pain relief sedated state could be part of our family interactions of speech so it could fall peacefully to her still functional hearing.

In certain parts of my mother's vigil, I would take aspects out as part of my mental resolve, in such harrowing surroundings with the ward itself housing four other seriously ill women, comforting moments would arise. One such segment of time was when the sounds emitting from radio waves that we were playing softly around my mother's bedside, brought a unity to the place of hurt and suffering. As the song in question went through the renditions of its chorus, a shushing gesture was made by one of my brothers, to bring us all to the attention what was happening outside the curtained-off borders of our given privacy.

The gentle melody had floated around to the occupants of the other beds and to the nursing staff in attendance. These unknowing choristers were reciting the lyrics of the song in a gentle soothing harmony as one, the song in question was Doris Day's *Que Sera, Sera*. This unique ambience I will cherish forever.

My mum's final hours would be in the privacy of her own room surrounded by her husband, myself, my wife and my two younger brothers. As I had done for the past seventy-two hours, I looked closely at my mum's slowing breathing, her intakes of breath, the gap widening very gradually, but the aura around the room was that there was still something she wished before the light shone bright to her.

My mum's last intention was realised, her purpose for the clinging onto this world by my wife suggesting that my older brother should be contacted by phone to say his final goodbyes to his mother, with his own reasons of not being able to attend personally, which father and siblings understood, the telephone contact was made.

With the one-way vocal goodbye beautifully conducted by my mum's firstborn, twenty minutes later, my mother's shallow breathing that was indicated by the rate the blanket we had lovingly chose to cover her in her last days stopped its rise up then down upon her chest, with the intense prolonged stare at the deep red blanket settling peacefully. My mum had passed beautifully with all her nearest and dearest at her side.

I use the term beautifully passed because this was the first time I had seen the ending of life in its natural way. Amongst the most upsetting experiences one could witness, the passing of a parent, yes, but my mother was fortunate to live to the life expectancy of a human being in the developed world.

I had only ever witnessed the taking of life prematurely on numerous occasions, not just witnessing but to be affected by life being prematurely taken away on so many other occasions.

Seeing my mother pass, in some sort of way helped me look at death in a different perspective. I had only ever experienced life ending first hand in a murderously evil unnatural form, leaving behind visions for myself to struggle and comprehend, but in a sort of therapeutic way, my mum was still helping me to her very last breath.

Chapter Twenty-Three
Inner Resolving

Inner resolve, a huge task for me, that I have battled with for decades, looking for the answers down dead ends, looking out into the landscape of hope to find disappointment, the fight that is fought on a daily basis by myself, is against myself.

My ideology from being young was it was certain persons, certain happenings that were my enemies, but it was myself and how I dealt with these people and situations that was really the major obstacle.

At some point in time, the mental strength of every individual will be tested to the limit, levels of trauma can be brushed off by some, affected greatly by others.

The atrocities seen on a daily basis by civilians in war-torn parts of the world would consider my experiences that I have labelled traumatic, tame. The human response can be one of being desensitised to such horrific events or losses, it becomes normal to see the abnormal.

I found the mental assault course of life a little harder to deal with, the way I am wired up if you like, a demeanour, a personality unique to every individual past and present; mine, I lock horns everyday with and always will.

For stability and possibly permanent recovery in the future, analysing my weaknesses, and there are to my own admission many, I stripped down what instigators had a route cause in stirring my rudder into turbulent thoughts and actions.

The wonderful innovations of the times we live in, the power that is held in the palm of our hand, a smart phone, technology that now even outweighs what the instrument panel on the flight deck of the early space shuttle missions could demonstrate, but that same device in your pocket can also infiltrate every one's life, track and traced on social media, performed or acted out falsely in front of you, portraying idyllic lifestyles, conjuring up thoughts of why yours is nothing of the sorts triggering negative responsive thoughts, I am well aware devices and such networks can also be of great help to mental insecurities, the balance is a delicate one.

Inter actions with people in general, I have took it upon myself to whittle away the non-essential types of engagement of acquaintances who paraded under the guise as a friend.

This in fact has made a big impact on my stability, drastic, not really, if everyone took a step back and thought who really held positive interests in your well-being not just an interest to benefit themselves, was really quite shocking in my instance.

At the top of the list of my daily mood lifting antidotes are my dogs. Without my four-legged best friends, things would have been a whole lot different, the giving of endless amounts of love and companionship with no strings attached, devotion unparallel, the calming stroke or pat scientifically proven to relieve stress and lower blood pressure, the benefits have been overwhelming.

With my two senior dogs suffering the inevitable effects of ageing, Bungie my eldest and named in memory of my best friend Rob, is now totally blind and deaf, but with his ever-faithful sense of smell, will spring into his playing posture on recognising I am in his company, coupled with his greeting of a hundred licks to the face.

Phoebe, this resilient little madam with idiopathic epilepsy, who has battled the effects of a stroke recently, is still the matriarch of the pack, which includes her two sons Junior and Brody.

Their now complete reliance for me to carry the two elders upstairs, to administer specific timed doses of medication throughout the day, is a privilege to give back some of the unconditional love they gave me in the times when I needed carrying in a different way, when human company of judgement would be the source of most of my despondencies.

My daily dose of medicating exercise is fundamental to a lean muscular train of thought, the same physical aspirations I am afraid are just that little bit harder to obtain, the mental ones I can flex more readily.

Eating the correct foods at the correct intervals can have a major impact towards a better state of mind greatly. A regime of educated eating, bespoke to yourself and your lifestyle I found to be the most successful.

Diet, a word of conflicting interpretation to a lot of people, to some means hell, starvation, irritable moods and ultimately failure to hit a targeted numerical figure of an ideal, approached in the more adopted form, for the purpose of longevity not a passing fad to failure, will prove to be more successful.

From past experience, the changing of food structuring can have effects towards positive stepping stones to better mental health, the obvious is of course weight loss, a better sustained energy output another, instead of the lethargic effects of an uneducated or a more rash approach of eating blind or comfort eating associated when in a bad state of mental health.

Eating for comfort can accelerate poor mental health in the way alcohol and drugs can, that elusive search for pleasure, euphoria. The architect dopamine is what we experience when our taste buds recognise something delicious, our primal instincts working in all their glory, that dangling carrot to entice the survival of our species, to eat.

Saying all this, I am still guilty on occasions now of not following my own guidelines to a better or prolonged quality of thinking. Under no circumstances am I free of irrational thoughts, contributing to a bout of depression, or irresponsible actions, but I am getting better at recognising the signs before they take hold, like they did in the past.

As I come to the conclusion of the documenting of my personal memoirs, an undertaking of which I started well before the latter chapters of the book happened, in fact, it has been a three- and half-year project for it to come to any sort of conclusion.

To summon up the courage in certain excerpts, to relive and tell them, to put myself personally under the microscope for myself to scrutinise, honestly and transparently as possible, has been hard to face up to. The only way to have accurately described these situations was to revisit them in my mind vividly again.

There were times when the emotions due to the self-imposed time travel of the mind disabled me into floods of tears, when the keyboard of my laptop resembled the unwiped draining board of a sink.

Thoughts that were not so welcome to enter into my mind, had to be enticed, braved, thus bringing emotions fitting to the thought emerging into a vision, anger, fear, hatred, love, all would pay a visit systematically, some repeatedly.

To some extent, the actual undertaking of my page-by-page accounts of health and ill health of the mind, reading back through them, there has developed a pattern of recovery repeatedly prevailing when but in place, the collapse of such recovery, again centres generally on the same narratives throughout my downturns of relapse into mental despair.

In a positive therapeutic view point, I have come to realise that the writing down, starting from scratch as a self-written autobiography if you like, analysing my own behaviour, I would say has helped me no ends in the stabilising of my condition.

On the passing of my mother, I recovered a preserved diary wrote by my mum, dating back fifty years; it documented the struggle she had with post-natal depression after giving birth to myself and the mood-changing effects of the menopause, which the daily entrants to the little book must have in some way, helped her overcome her struggles by detailing her emotions in the personal memoirs regarding her mental health.

The sad statistics of a person becoming a victim from the fatal effects of bad mental health is worryingly growing. Four personal friends in the last ten years have taken their own lives. I never reacted to the warnings or their subtle cries for help from one friend in particular; the youngest was in their early twenties, the oldest being middle aged. I still see the devastating effects fatal mental illness has had on their families with them not being alive no more.

On the flipside, talking to people in my coaching capacity, the recovery from despair through the effects of exercise is encouraging knowing this is a platform, or like myself a medication to stimulate that happy neurotransmitter serotonin.

A philosophy that works for me is to RUN WHEN YOU'RE NUMB. In my worst ever times of despair, as I have documented during the past chapters, running has been my go-to relief. I'm not a naturally gifted athlete, believe me, you don't have to be, every human being's evolved to run, from being hunter and gatherers, that's why we have an Achilles tendon most other mammals don't.

Try it, if you feel them storm clouds rolling in, slip on any type of reasonable footwear (I don't mean stilettos, then again I haven't tried a pair, then again I think I might've in one of my deluded state of minds), they don't have to be the most fashionable or the most high-tech pair of trainers, don't wait, just run, very slow, fast, 2 minutes or two hours, rain, sun, day or night, doesn't matter, just run; it worked for me at my most desperate and lowest periods of my life.

Covid-19,
Editing in Isolation
(Impromptu Entry 1)

As I begin to undertake the editing period of these memoirs, the world has resided in a very unsettling period of time in its human inhabitancy: the pandemic that is the Coronavirus – COVID-19.

As I sit at my desk on the fourth week of compulsory isolation, the devastating march of this dreadful virus continues, putting the lives of us all on hold, even worse, ending the lives of so many others.

Literally, as I press the buttons on my laptop to document this impromptu entry, a local news bulletin on TV highlights the other worry now becoming the other concern of lockdown: mental health.

The suicide of a young teenager during the government-imposed lockdown headlines the programme, with the prediction from the parent of the young girl a very realistic one, that it certainly won't be the last due to the new unexpected mental burdens of isolation.

With the growing number of fatalities from the virus, with it the growing number of bereaved families increases, the restrictions of the normal grieving process, the actual attendance at the stricken person's bedside not allowed, the limited gathering at funerals, sets the perfect environment for mental health issues to multiply. Just like the COVID-19 virus found the right conditions to thrive, so will the decline of a healthy mindset.

My own father himself contracting the virus, taken from his care home by ambulance, a two-week period of not knowing what his condition was because of the strict policies at the hospital on non-visiting, an extreme anxious worrying timeline prevailed, the same as with so many other families.

My father with the superb help of our great doctors and nurses of our NHS recovered from the virus, not like so many at his age with the same underlining health conditions.

This was clearly evident on hearing such a sad tale of the times, my eldest brother hearing through the brick walls of his home the uncontrollable sobs of sorrow from his neighbour, when she had been told of her own mother's demise to the virus, her sorrow itself having to been dealt with alone due to her own isolation. Truly heart-breaking.

Covid-19 (Impromptu Entry 2)

My attention again is to focus upon another impromptu entry, this added account I write just a few days after the above paragraphs were submitted into my memoirs and again is a reflection of a changed and quite cruel timeline my family, like so many others, have had to endure.

After a victorious last battle won with the virus named COVID-19, given the all clear due to the non-appearance of problematic symptoms one week previous, a phone call from the frontline of heroines locking horns, keeping the march of the big disease with a smaller abbreviated name at bay, my father's care home delivered the usual isolated update of my dad's condition.

In one of those moments dreaded by any offspring, a younger brother listened to the analysis to my father's worsening condition from one of the dedicated unsung heroines of this dire time.

A cruel decision now by us brothers had to be undertook, the option of sending my father back into the savages of battle into hospital, where he unfortunately contracted the enemy but fortunately prevailed in victory, or on advice from the attending district nurse and own appointed doctor to just reduce the warrior's now fatigued battle-ravaged pains and irritability of illness.

Both choices had heart-breaking consequences for the siblings. Unlike my mother's bedside vigil fifteen months previous, the same form of comforting for my father and his sons was not possible, cruelly taken away from the family down to the indiscriminate contagiousness of COVID-19 in such the environment a care home presented to the vulnerable residents, the same circumstances on hospitalisation.

The comfort and familiar surroundings of his trusted care home was decided to be the location of settling down and resting after the gargantuan battles of the last fifteen months with the passing of his inseparable partner that was my mother, three debilitating strokes, two heart attacks, six bouts of pneumonia and the final W recorded on his fight record COVID-19.

I myself would be the appointed lone prohibited member of the brothers to attend his bedside, due to the strict conditions of isolation, the post type apocalyptic car journey of a deserted motorway due to the imposed stay-at-home government restrictions, made the proposed aimed destination that much more intimidating.

On my arrival, this solo attendance to enter the care home had its strict stipulations of entrance, to don the armour now routinely worn by the masses of the frontline all over the world, face mask, surgical gloves and a plastic apron covering for the body.

Reassuring words of comfort for the last big push for eternal peace were the encouraged battle plans as I sat at my dad's bedside, as a concoction of relaxants were injected into his arm to induce a more comfortable night's rest.

The laying down of arms, the white flag of surrender options, but not just yet, as my father's own crumbling body's city walls were under a ruthless assault from the unforgiving armies of old age, with the last toe-to-toe battle with COVID-19 taking its toll, the signifying gesture of a retirement from the fight would be done on his own terms, his way.

A change of plan was now put in place by the astonished medical personnel on the morning of the next day, realising the resilience of their charge, the predicted last final days would be backed up by the reinforcements in the form of hospitalisation, a return to the more equipped regiment of palliative care would be the last stand.

APRIL 27th 2020

The criteria of the third day in the surroundings of the tender loving care of the professionals would present the solo return by myself due to the understandable but nevertheless cruel policies that COVID-19 has enforced.

The remaining brothers still side-lined to attend due to the high risk factors of contamination, a cruel denial of the times subjected to many a family.

Entering the epicentre, the eye of the storm to see first-hand what others were unaware of, the positive energy, the exhausting effort of a fight in mid-flight by all NHS staff.

The importance of each one now on an even keel, the attention to detail of a cleaner now in line with that of a degree held by a doctor from medical school, as they all swim in the infested waters of the deadly virus together.

It rammed home to me what no news bulletin or a newspaper report could put across in its severity of the situation that was bestowed on the world.

The obligatory PPE defences donned yet again, the generous application of hand sanitizer, absorbing into the dry cracked skin of the fingers, the stinging a reminder of its constant recent liberal use.

A rightful use of innovative communicating technology in the form of a smart phone provided the screened presence for absent siblings, as testimonies to my father's grateful parenting were heartfelt and lovingly relayed to him.

One by one, recognising the signs that retiring from the battle was near, final goodbyes and a thank you were tearfully submitted.

As little children, myself and my older brother would excitedly accompany our dad on our weekend morning or evening walk to Jimmy Johnson's newspaper emporium situated on the crescent at the top of our road.

The front window of which would display sun-faded items like lucky bags, a cardboard plinth displaying pocket pen knifes, next to that an array of smoking pipes and an Action Man imitation, an inferior replica mimicking the more lucrative boys' toy of the time, for the older generation a copy of *Women's Own* or *Shoot*, a weekly magazine for the football enthusiast of any age.

All would be surrounded on the base of the display by blue bottles which had perished in the heat of the south-facing shop front to create a fly's graveyard, which the resident spider would feast on the rich pickings at will, seemingly getting ever bigger on each one of our shop window browsing visits.

The short trundle was for the usual purchase of my dad's weekend reads of duvet-sized Sunday newspapers or the Saturday evening edition of the equally sized pink *Liverpool Football Echo*.

More importantly for us would be of our own choice of prized sweets, Jelly Tots being my usual chosen option, a bag of colourful Tooty Frooties was my brother David's pick, but the highlight of this short journey was the insistence for our dad to give me and my brother a 'swingy'.

Holding mine and my brother's hands either side of him, with a firm grip, he would swing us both high up into the sky.

It was now my time to return the favour as I held his hand lovingly on his last breath taken, the momentum of my handheld swingy ascending him up to the heavenly skies in which his spirit would continue the journey onwards.

One last look at my dad peacefully at rest, gleaming, immaculate the way I knew him as, thanks to the palliative skills to his personal appearance from nurses, I would exit the fortress of hospital walls, shielding inhabitants from the advance of the virus, at the same time battling it with patients already infected, a fourteen-day self-isolation period was now imposed upon myself.

The consoling hug and needed emotional support of siblings comforting each other outside the rotating doors of the hospital was denied, holding the top of a roadside rail and leaning on the shoulder of my wife would instead support my limp body weight.

At a distance of two metres apart, visual tearful embraced condolences were agonisingly observed with my youngest sibling, his lone vigil conducted from the car park, two other brothers not even allowed to cross their own doorway due to their lack of immunity, due to the suppressing side-effects of medication being taken.

Vigil rights with the last sensory touch of a goodbye to their father, had been ripped away from them all, another teasing poke from the bully that had the whole world in a head lock, again the cruel reality of the times prevailing.

Covid-19
(Impromptu entry 3)

Back to lockdown and even stricter isolation for myself, mourning would have to be self-contained. No visits to the house I grew up in, no drive-bys past my Nana's old house, Daisy Street, Kirkdale, near the city centre, the childhood home of my father, thus to help me with the grieving process.

Instead, a paint brush with all the other decorating accessories, my own therapeutic form of poignant mourning, my dad a painter and decorator by trade, skills of which he taught me as a young boy.

"Spread the paint about, then feather it off lightly."

The words of his tuition still sounding in my ears like it was yesterday.

The sunlight of the day cast a shadow of my face onto the wall, the wall that was about to be covered with the cookie dough coloured emulsion of choice.

My silhouetted outline was identical to the face of my father which I had stared tearfully at while his pathway for passing was built days before at his hospital bedside.

It was if my dad was still looking over my shoulder, observing his son's tentative cutting in prowess with the bristles of the brush, in an acceptance of his presence, a smile and that extra bit of attention to detail not to disappoint.

Covid-19
(Impromptu Entry 4)

Born under the threat of a tyrant, whose squadrons of the Luftwaffe rained hell from the skies above Liverpool in the Blitz of 1941, surviving these relentless bombardments, my father's life would end 79 years later, the world under threat again by another tyrant, the Coronavirus epidemic.

Surviving its initial bombardment but his already weakened foundations eventually crumbling after the raid on my father's now fragile immune system.

Just like a controversial decision from a panel of judges in a boxing match, COVID-19 had its hand raised unlawfully as my father became another statistic in its relentless march of destruction, its abbreviated name unrightfully being placed on his death certificate.

Conditions, restrictions, distancing, not words usually used in respect to a funeral, but this is the reality of the world living through a pandemic.

Social distancing totally nullifies the role the outpouring of grief and the need to mourn for a loved one, that a funeral service and gathering provides for relatives and friends.

The peripheral aftershocks of COVID-19 still very much apparent as it was when its crowned microscopic guise destroyed the branches of the oxygen-seeking lungs of its chosen victim.

Mourners restricted to no more than 10 at the funeral service, seating rows of pews removed, replaced with single individual seats spaced two metres apart.

A sibling's agonisingly cruel absence, his acute vulnerability again highlighted, exposure to the invisible threat could well present a similar ceremony but with him as the centre piece.

Eulogy delivered again as was his goodbye to his father at his hospital bedside by the technology of the present day, one-dimensional, on screen, but spiritually and emotionally very much multi-dimensional.

Myself and my youngest brother sat 2 metres apart at our Father's funeral in 2020 after his passing from COVID 19, near enough to the day the UK government gathered in the garden of number 10 observing no social distancing rules what so ever

The gulf between two siblings measured at two metres, feeling more in miles than the metric distance allowed.

Social distancing, isolation, these words took a new meaning to me as me and my brother wept alone sat staring at my father's coffin before its committal journey began.

The simple wrapping warmth of an arm or the holding of a hand for comfort or support would have been highly desirable to bolster our emotionally ravaged states of mind but cruelly outlawed.

The service condensed to a meagre twenty or so minutes during which time sitting on the moon would not have felt less isolated.

No gathering of family and friends in the wake of the proceedings, straight home to play a cherished recovered collection of vinyl – '45s and '33s – from the now empty house of my childhood home, each piece once playing delivering cascades of memories in music, replacing the discussions of by-gone times with relatives and friends a wake usually provides, and admittedly doing a great job, also safe guarding my own mental health, also doing a great job.

As these last few impromptu entries testify, our mental strength is being put a lot more to the test much more frequently. A lot of uncertainties have manifested themselves in our daily lives as we try to forecast the future, a future that can only shine bright if you safeguard your mental health, in turn physical health has a better chance to follow.

By detailing my own experiences of variable mental health, it has helped me realise simple antidotes or to be aware to prevention of any infestations of negative thought, in most instances irrational like a burrowing worm once deep routed the reasoning for such unjust thinking can be devastating.

Sympathetic listening a life saver even, simplistic concerning communication in the form of a text can carry the embrace of a hug or a hand to hold through the waves of technology.

My own relationship with social media and smart phones has simmered in the light of the COVID-19 pandemic, the realisation that it can also be a friend as well as foe, the networks and technology providing a source of extreme comfort for families and friends separated in these trying times offsetting openings for the darkened diversity of thought.

Some say talk is cheap, but talking can also be priceless. Words CAN speak louder than actions.

In my lifetime of searching, solace has been sought by me in an easy read version of a certain book, especially at these trying times, first thing in the morning, also during parts of the day when the need to reach out becomes more intense and most welcoming.

The new part of this book is actually over two thousand years old. Out of all the literature I have undertook, all the research available online, I have read nothing that comes close to a source of understanding, comfort and teaching into how to cope with your inner troubled soul. It can be found in every good book store and usually in the top draw of a good hotel.

The Bible.

As for myself now, well, I am nurturing, learning and trying to observe my newfound faith as a Christian and my relationship with God.

My faith has allowed me to do what I thought after doctors told me I would not do again, and that is to run, regardless of the pain, it's a coping mechanism and the only truly successful medication, proven to have helped me in the past.

Just before my dad passed away, as I sat holding his hand in a hospital ravaged by the pandemic, I prayed to God like most people do in times of grief, thanking him for the life of my father and promising my dad I will stay strong no matter what, so I took off my leg braces virtually straightaway after his passing, thus enabling me to shake off the shackles debilitating the way I wanted to live and needed to live life.

Yes, the pain without them was there, but over time slowly it abated to a point where I could tolerate the discomfort, so an attempt at a little trot gathered pace. 6 months in after hitting the trails once again with my two able running dogs and a lot of morning and evening prayer, I am three stone lighter, my addiction to pain killers beaten and the use of high blood pressure medication ceased; my blood pressure according to my monitor, I now have the readings of a thirty-year-old.

This hope and reassurance given to me by the grace of God that's slowly solidifying my mental and physical state, didn't happen overnight admittedly, but manifested over a period of time starting from when I forecasted in my head that inevitable dark times lay ahead, this time purely because of the lifespan of loved ones concluding naturally.

I really thought long and hard how my frail mental state could cope with such losses, so just before my mum passed, I started reading the Bible. It was a hard read to grasp at first. Slowly, prayer became a more often occurrence in my day.

My prediction was correct with the passing of my parents and very recently one of my precious dogs Phoebe, the little tenacious Boston Terrier passing in my wife's arms peacefully after 13 years 8 months of loyalty and devotion.

My faith certainly brought a shielding defence from my demons that in the past carried me off when facing them toe to toe, a war I often came second best in.

THE HARDEST OF ALL IMPROMPTU ENTRIES

I now once again switch on my laptop to add what I have been calling impromptu entries into my memoirs.

These particular paragraphs of explanation come truly to myself the hardest yet to document. As explained in past pages, my prophecy of fatalities due to the expiration timelines of a natural lifespan led me to my new faith. The faith in which I have immersed myself in is now under a severe test with a microscopic form of scrutiny and a questioning of why.

My eldest brother David Paul Scott who helps envisage and encourages me to build a picture in this book of two young boys growing up in a carefree world, whose only cares then being the competitive spirit of children at play.

Examples brought to the readers' attention on that long hot summer's day in the late seventies in Chapter One, the only concerns of who would be victorious in that makeshift squared ring, coupled with the throwing of a ping pong ball into empty glass jam jars.

A world that gradually opens up to the realities of life that are not so caring and fancy free, as young teenagers thrusted into the defence of their family and homestead from a cowardly, bullying predator in Chapter Four.

Like a vicious rally between two ace tennis players, David's courageous battle against his invisible tormentors came to an abrupt, tragic and totally unnecessary end. Only 16 months my senior, my first idol, my first super hero is found heartbreakingly lifeless on the floor of his apartment by my two younger siblings, at the age of 53.

After 50 years of mutual caring of our parents and my parents for him, the time had come because of their passing 15 months apart to have his own independence.

As a young adult, David started to exhibit traits of the condition Asperger's syndrome, a part of the autism spectrum. Through encouragement from his three younger brothers, he agreed to seek the confirmation and hopefully a diagnosis of his suspected condition after my parents passed away.

Incredibly, that diagnosis to sit in front of a panel of Asperger's professionals would absurdly be SEVEN years, yes, SEVEN, that is the length of time waiting for an appointment for an Asperger's test would've took, David only managed TWO of those seven years before a diagnosis became futile due to his untimely death.

Again, I talk about getting let down by the health authorities, David unquestionably was victim to numerous failings from these bodies. The end of lockdown during the summer of 2021 with someone who suffers with a social interaction problem that Asperger's is, only worsened the condition to a point of total unequivocal self-isolation even after the so-called Freedom Day in June 2021.

Masking the condition like in so many other people's lives, like my own even, David sought solace in the tin cylinder shaped vessel that held the contents of a self-prescribed antidote, in the form of alcohol, that again like so many self-help remedies became another tormentor to my brother's overall well-being, but if the persistence of a condition that plagues you goes untreated by twenty-first-century medicine and expertise, and a short-term remedy is available to you sitting on the shelves of every corner shop, the temptation is just too much to overcome.

My brother fought and was overcoming nicely from his go-to when battling with his extreme anxieties to face social interaction, when a fatal unprecedented final let-down presented itself.

On feeling decisively unwell, with advise from myself and my youngest brother, ourselves unable at that time to go to his apartment he rang the 999 emergency services for an ambulance to take him to hospital, or at the very least to give him an onsite assessment of the symptoms he was exhibiting.

The estimated time of arrival was to be in a thirteen hour time frame as the North West ambulance service deemed my brother's demeanour over the phone as non life threatening coupled with the lack of response vehicles available, but they would attend to him sooner rather than later.

It was my two younger brothers, out of now worrying concern to go around to David's flat after having no joy trying to communicate with him, more than twenty hours after the first initial phone call for help from David the North West ambulance service did not just arrive on time, they never attended at all.

The grim heartbreaking discovery of David's lifeless body was made by my two younger siblings, the next tearful emotionally charged phone call to the emergency services was for an ambulance to pick up David's body…

Ironically to pick up a dead body, that took just twenty minutes for an ambulance to arrive.

We can all argue what was right and wrong with the UK's Government's response to the COVID 19 pandemic, but the truth of the matter is, near enough to the day of my father's funeral, were only ten family members could attend, as I sat two metres away from my youngest brother not able to console each other, our UK Government and staff were attending a garden party in the grounds of number 10, observing no social distance rules what so ever, in which attending persons were made accountable and fined including our own Prime Minister.

With the self-isolation chaos still in place in 2021, this policy placed all our emergency services into being under staffed and into disarray, with generally healthy staff willing to work but not being able to because of this ruling of self-isolation, this in turn cost lives, one of them being my brother's.

The days preceding my older brother's passing, my go-to, the donning of my running attire, hitting the trails with my beloved dogs, again came to my rescue.

Previously I wrote about to run when you're numb as a form of therapy, this time was different, I was paralysed.

Tears mingled with the accumulation of sweat coming from the pores of my face, saturating it as if I had been caught in a torrential downpour, yet I was in a storm, the eye of a heart-breaking emotional one, a category five.

Lifting my head up to the heavens as I plodded aimlessly along the uneven farmer's path, my dogs harnessed to me, aiding the pull to their non-motivated attached but mentally detached weight, I bellowed, "WHY?!" out loud, totally unconcerned or unaware if there was any presence of anyone else around. There was a presence and always had been, like an older brother's concerned worry for his younger sibling, a powerful spiritual voice of guidance came suddenly through the ear phones from my music playing device, in a piece of music so apt for the moment.

Clinging on now to every lyric sung hitting my ear canal composed from the unmistakeable iconic, somewhat appropriate brotherly partnership of the Gallaghers, the words from their collaboration levitating me into a calming transfixed bubble of fixation.

HOLD UP
HOLD ON
YOU'LL NEVER CHANGE WHAT'S BEEN AND GONE

MAY YOUR SMILE
SHINE ON
DON'T BE SCARED
YOUR DESTINY MAY KEEP YOU WARM

'CAUSE ALL THE STARS ARE FADING AWAY
JUST TRY NOT TO WORRY YOU'LL SEE THEM SOME DAY
TAKE WHAT YOU NEED, AND BE ON YOUR WAY
AND STOP CRYING YOUR HEART OUT

The music acted as if it was an interpreter, relaying its message from its spiritual origin; to me that original source was David, my older concerned brother, with comforting tones of reassurance, very much helped his hurting younger brother come through the relentless battering of emotional climatology of grief.

Our Boston Terriers past and present, undoubtedly were and still play a huge part in my mental health stability

It's mystifyingly unimaginable that I write about another strain of mental illness, and a seemingly preventable death, that of my brother's, what the whole world has endured in recent years, it's not surprising that statistics of deaths sky-rocketing not just from COVID-19 attacking the respiratory system but from the safeguards that were supposed to protect the population, isolation, it has also and still is claiming lives.

Myself and younger brothers beckon for answers to that question WHY, the question I shouted to the heavens on that dusty farmer's path, but for the time being that will have to wait. Internal and external investigations are under way by the official authorities, which does not come as any form of reconciliation to ourselves as the internal emotions run wildly out of control in, are now one-tracked train of thought.

Effective safeguards are now at a high level to protect the vulnerable state of mind bereavement cloaks over your soul, as if all the previous times, the failures, the not-so-effective formulas of shielding from hurt and confusion had all been trial runs until a successful remedy could be used in such dire circumstances, like the heart-wrenching one we find ourselves in. This one has an added destructive emotion thrown into the mix – anger.

My war like pointing finger hovers over the suspects of neglect, it jabs powerfully in my mind wanting the guilty party to stand up and be made accountable, to tame this beast hasn't been easy for me in the past.

The blockade, checkpoints, the sentries on duty to serve and protect, being my faith, the numb runs in the countryside with my guardian four-legged companions both acting like an impenetrable defence system shepherding away the barraging devilment of irrational thought.

Grief has an overwhelming array of powers. Everyone will experience raw primal grief at some point in their life. Experiencing this emotion on numerous occasions, condensed in a short period of time prompted me to run numb every day, regardless of the bone-on-bone grinding of my knees, that pain paled into insignificance the chaos of thought that was accumulating in my brittle observations of life. After my brother David passed away, I realised the dream of running a marathon again was in my grasp without really knowing it, so I put this by-product of sheer grief to use.

David, who was waiting for an assessment on the Autism Spectrum at the time of his death, I decided to run the Liverpool Marathon for Autism Initiatives nine and a half weeks after his passing.

The channelled power of faith and grief masks the pain you have elsewhere in your body, so I took up the challenge on the 24/10/2021. I crossed the finish line in 4 hours 9 minutes on the iconic docklands with a plethora of emotions, grief still the governor followed by in no particular order, pride and an abundance of memories of my brother, prompting tears to again trickle down my salt-dried face of a marathon finisher. Family and friends raised an amazing £1495 for Autism Initiatives in David's memory.

There was also one more surfacing emotion poking around my crowded thought channels, an anxiety, to brace myself for another traumatising period of my life I was dreading so much, losing my little saviour, my best ever friend and companion, my precious little Boston Terrier Bungie.

Days before the marathon, the realisation that time was running out for Bungie had to be faced. Actually pulling out of the marathon crossed my mind, time left with him was at that much of a premium now and I didn't want to leave him for any extended period of time.

Four days after the marathon, Bungie the little dog, who and I have no reservations about writing this, saved my life and changed the lives of so many over the years in one way or another, I sat with him in the very same place, lying on me in the same way he did on that very first day as a trembling little ball of fur, as the incredible bond formed when I brought him back to his new home as puppy 14 years 7 months previous, I held him to the very last beat of his heart, a heart that was only filled with a devotion and love for his human adopted family as he passed away peacefully.

From the moment I picked him out amongst the other adorable pups from the litter, there wasn't a question in my mind he was the dog I was destined to take home. Bungie as previously mentioned was named after my best friend Rob who passed away so very prematurely. After such a traumatic and gigantic loss, I sought out comfort through the companionship of man's best friend.

Many other people after seeing Bungie introduced Boston Terriers into their families and so it spread, the love and happiness, never more so when him and Phoebe had puppies themselves. We witnessed first-hand their precious brood transform the lives of their new owners just like how our Bostons were a revelation to ours.

Maybe only dog owners can comprehend how much our dogs play a part in making life that much more bearable in times when human participation or intentions have been wrong or questionable.

Bungie came into my life when I needed added reassurances that life was worth living. He left me ironically when at that moment in time. I'm now in a more stable, sustainable and have never been more in control of my ever-inconsistent mental health.

It was as if he was my guardian angel sent to me in my time of need and wouldn't leave till his job was done, totally blind and deaf for the last three years of his life, but still equipped with his mightiest of assets, his nose. He knew exactly who was in the room at any one time and never let his other failed senses dampen his zest for life and the love for his family.

Just like a dog that changes the life of a visually impaired person, Bungie the Boston Terrier was my own guide dog, a guide dog that navigated me around the many obstacles that life put in front of me. He helped me cross those unforgiving roads of depression, stopping at the curbs in my mind, making me wait till it was safe for me to cross.

The amalgamation, the knitted infusion of faith intertwined with the proven methods of stability, has provided me with progression and a mentality of defiance against the short circuits of thought I can so often be bombarded by. I finally accept those attacks and am willing to go head to head in a damn good fisticuffs with them. Yes, at last I think I have found the elusive pot of gold within myself to stand up to the inner me that was so unfit and lacking the essential cerebral fitness needed to survive in the ups and downs of life.

The fight continues, the fight with me is for life, because that fight IS with what we call LIFE itself – fragile, chaotic, turbulent, happy and sad, oh so brief, but forever so very precious…

VINCIT QUI SE VINCIT, is my motto – HE CONQUERS WHEN HE CONQUERS HIMSELF.

So on that note, seconds out, ding, ding, let the next round commence.
Thank You.
God Bless.